Faith in the furnace

Understanding God's purpose in the trials of life

© Ian Rees 2006
First printed 2006

ISBN 978-1-84625-045-3

9 781846 250453 >

British Library Cataloguing in Publication Data available

Published by Day One Publications
Ryelands Road, Leominster, HR6 8NZ
☎ 01568 613 740 FAX 01568 611 473
email—sales@dayone.co.uk
web site—www.dayone.co.uk
North American—e-mail—sales@dayonebookstore.com
North American—web site—www.dayonebookstore.com

Designed by Steve Devane and printed by Gutenberg Press, Malta

To my parents
David and Joan Rees
With thanks for their unfailing encouragement

Contents

This book will equip you for the trials that come your way. It is easy to read, very well illustrated and most of all opens up the Scriptures on the massive problems we all face from time to time. Seldom have modern writers displayed such ability to make their work so easy to read, practical and, at the same time, utterly faithful to the Word of God. Those who read this book will thank God for it and those who preach will soon be quoting from it. I hope we will get more from Ian Rees' pen very soon.

Chris Kelly
Minister of Lansdowne Baptist Church, Bournemouth, England

In *Faith in the Furnace,* Ian Rees tackles some of the most perplexing questions that Christians face. You may ask, 'Do we need another book about suffering?' Positive thinkers may say, 'No!' but realists, among whom serious Christians make up a large proportion, will affirm its necessity. Tragedies, cancer, obdurate pain and untimely death raise such vexing questions that we need all the help we can get. An important facet of Christian discipleship involves storing in the closets of our minds the resources we will need to face the inevitable trials that will threaten our faith. In that regard, I would commend Ian Rees for his helpful addition to this genre.

Rees approaches the subject in an approachable style that leaves us with an understandable and very practical array of resources. His biblical exposition is fresh and illuminating. Throughout, he seasons the vital principles he extracts from the Word with real stories. He uses a wide array of helpful sources and ranges broadly over the whole subject of how to maintain one's faith in the midst of trials. This book is not a single-issue book, dealing—for example—with the loss of a loved one or the sudden diagnosis of a deadly cancer. He deals with suffering from many perspectives: the suffering of delay, disappointment with God, the silence of God, the darkness of despair, handling setbacks, dealing with the sufferings of the innocent, betrayal, and facing the approach of death. He also handles well the deadly effects of prosperity.

Eric E Wright
Author of five books, including *Revolutionary Forgiveness*, the editor of *the Fellowship LINK* magazine, and a semi-retired pastor and missionary, Ontario, Canada

Faith in the Furnace is a book that explains basic but deep issues of the Christian life that we never actually grow beyond, and explains them biblically, in a lively manner, with engaging illustrations peppered from church history, missionary activity, pastoral work, and the contemporary scene. Ian Rees deals with the very practical themes of Christian discipleship in a biblical, pastoral and contemporary way.

This is an ideal book to give to new disciples who are familiar with the pop-culture of today, but who need grounding in sound biblical principles. Yet it would also be of great benefit to disciples of a few years' maturity who need to understand afresh the experiences and changing scenes of the life they pass through. With solid and deep exegesis from the biblical text, here is a theology of discipleship based on the Bible, rather than just on the themes of the Bible.

Paul Pease
Author and Pastor of Hook Evangelical Church, Surbiton, Surrey, England

Ian Rees has done all who follow Jesus in this confused and confusing world a great service with this book. He handles Scripture faithfully and his illustrative material sensitively so that the latter puts recognizable flesh and bones on familiar texts, bringing them to contemporary life and enabling them to encourage twenty-first-century followers of the Way as they deal with life. This book is easy to read but Mr Rees avoids offering the easy solutions that so many writers on this subject seem to feel modern Christians must have. We should thank him for taking us and our lives more seriously than that!

Stephen Gabbott BSc, ThL, BD, MA
Interim Vicar of Christ Church, Bangkok, previously of the Anglican Diocese of Sydney

How biblically healthy is our faith when tested in the furnace of affliction? Have western Christians come to expect largely trouble-free lives, and have we imbibed more of a health and wealth mindset than we realize?

With biblical realism Ian Rees examines the trials and pressures which modern Christians face in the light of God's ultimate aim for us, which is to mature us in Christ.

At times, the furnace is a place of vivid meeting with God, at others, a place of desolation and unanswered questions. This book helps us to see that either way, God is wisely and lovingly working to enrich our faith and make us 'as much like Jesus as it is possible to be this side of eternity'.

Ian writes with a refreshingly contemporary style and an engagement with the modern world. Clear biblical thinking is wedded to warm pastoral application through many telling illustrations and testimonies.

Bill Dyer
Minister of Pontefract Congregational Church (Evangelical), West Yorkshire, England

Part 1
Tried and tested—basic principles

1 Joy:
Songs in the prison cell

Finding the right note when responding to difficulty

What shall I say in this great day of the Lord, wherein in the midst of a cloud I have found a fair sunshine. I can wish no more for you but that the Lord may comfort you, and shine upon you as he does upon me, and give you that same sense of his love in staying in the world, as I have in going out of it (Scottish Covenanter, on the day of his execution[1]).

Please read Acts 16 and James 1:1–15.

I wonder if Paul and Silas could sing in harmony—perhaps Paul was the baritone, with Silas the tenor? Everything about their working relationship was harmonious, so why not this aspect, too? Imagine: they could have been the first-century equivalents of singers Bryn Terfel and Russell Watson, touring the Roman world and also planting churches. That is nothing more than day-dreaming, of course, but we do know that they sang together. Arrested in the Roman colony of Philippi for driving a demon out of a slave girl and thus depriving her owners of further income from her fortune-telling activities, they were severely beaten before being thrown into jail and chained up. But Luke, who wrote the account in Acts, tells us that that same night they were singing hymns at midnight, with the rest of the prisoners listening in (they probably didn't have much choice!). No mention of two-part harmonies, or even whether they were in tune or not, but their joyful singing in adversity not only indicates they were willing to practise what they preached (Paul says in Romans 5 that they rejoiced in sufferings), but also demonstrated what the appropriate Christian response to difficulty should be. This response has been a pattern that suffering Christians have followed ever since, and it is this that James has in view as he writes in verse 2 about the trials we face.

You need only travel a short way into Christian history to find people echoing Paul and Silas's double act. The whole band of apostles was arrested in the early days of the New Testament church for refusing to stop preaching, and all were beaten for their defiance. Their immediate reaction was joy that they had been counted worthy of suffering for Christ, a response that was tested to the full in subsequent years. Every one of them except John was, as far as we know, martyred for his faith. The early church willingly followed this trail laid down by the apostles, and the pattern repeats itself down the ages. It was said of the English martyrs of Queen Mary's reign that they went to their execution as if they were going to a wedding, but they are by no means exceptional. Whether you read *Foxe's Book of Martyrs*, which was written in the sixteenth century, or *Jesus Freaks* by dc Talk, which appeared at the end of the twentieth, you will encounter the same reaction to suffering. James' words hold the key to understanding how such a reaction is possible.

> Their immediate reaction was joy that they had been counted worthy of suffering for Christ.

Facing trials

Trials are, by definition, difficult circumstances that try or test you, not happy events. They stretch your faith in God to breaking point ('Has God forgotten me? Is he going to help me? How am I going to get out of this mess?'), but they do more than that. The double whammy trials land on you is that they also tempt you, perhaps to deny God or to do something that is wrong ('Forget God—he seems to have forgotten you. Go your own way'), and the original Greek of our word 'trials' reflects this dual meaning. In English we speak of two separate things, testing and temptation, with the first seen as positive and the second, negative. But the Greek text here uses a word which can have both meanings, and we have to decide which one to use, according to the context. Thus the noun used in verses 2 and 12 is translated as 'trials', while the related verb in verses 13 and 14 is rendered 'tempted'.

What James has in view, therefore, are difficult outward circumstances that are at the same time an inward source of temptation. It is this combination that makes trials what they are—trying. Pressured from the outside, you also find yourself pulled away from God from within, a process described with uncomfortable accuracy in James 1:13–15.

Something of the pain these trials cause is hinted at by James when he describes how they come our way. Some of the translations are rather tame when they speak of the trials we might 'face', when James really speaks of the trials we 'fall into'. The same word is used in the parable told by Jesus of the Good Samaritan to describe the fate of the unfortunate traveller who fell among thieves (Luke 10:25–37). Innocently travelling along the road from Jerusalem to Jericho he was set upon suddenly, robbed, beaten up and left for dead. Similarly for us, life may be smooth and pleasant at the moment, but storms can brew with astonishing speed: redundancy from work, illness or bereavement. A doctor my wife knew while she was training as a radiographer came into the department one day for a routine chest X-ray as part of a medical check-up he was having. He had no health problems or symptoms, but the X-ray revealed that his whole body was riddled with cancer and that he had little time left to live. Storms like this sweep down with a suddenness that threatens to swamp us or capsize the frail craft we are sailing in. It is this painful reality that James has in view.

> Storms can brew with astonishing speed.

Sudden disasters of that magnitude are, of course, not the norm in life, but trials are. There are many other different words in the Bible to describe the hardships we face—difficulties, afflictions, tribulations, persecutions, sufferings—all of them, like this one, pointing to the normality of such events. Peter tells his readers not to 'be surprised at the painful trial you are suffering, as though something strange were happening to you' (1 Peter 4:12), and neither should we be. James significantly does not say how to behave '*if* you face trials', but '*whenever*', indicating that trials, while they may not be our lot continually, are inevitable at some point and are part of the normal Christian life.

You don't have to look far to find some pretty desperate attempts at evading the impact of the obvious meaning of the Scriptures on this matter. I once came across an advertisement for a series of videos advocating riches for all believers and informing us that financial prosperity was God's will for everyone. There were phrases like 'getting into the stream of God's financial blessing' and 'God does not intend you to be poor.' The preacher's face was beaming out from the magazine, ready to receive your order, so he at least was going to be made richer through the videos. On a related issue—that of personal health—I have read explanations by sincere believers who could not accept that God's children should remain sick. I sympathize with the desire, but not the theology. All fail to see that the Bible has many words for difficulties and that poverty and sickness fall under the umbrella of those terms. You cannot isolate them from the list of traumas that may beset the believer and maintain that God will allow anything except these. God may deliver us from financial and health problems (in the West most of us are monumentally wealthy when compared with the rest of the world, so you could argue that he has done so already), but the normal Christian life unavoidably involves facing trials and, if God so chooses, poverty and sickness will be among them.

Smile?

The natural reaction to chronic afflictions is either to succumb to stoical resignation ('you've just got to grin and bear it') or to wallow in self-pity ('I've worked hard for this nervous breakdown, so I'm going to jolly well enjoy it'), but James will let us pursue neither of these options. Rather, he leaps straight in and tells us to view our situation as a cause for rejoicing: 'Consider it pure joy …' (v. 2).

> Trials, while they may not be our lot continually, are inevitable at some point and are part of the normal Christian life.

Joy? This appears worse than the options previously ruled out. It sounds like a crass recommendation for wearing a silly grin and pretending that reality is different ('smile long enough and your problems will go away'). Perhaps there are Christians who give the impression that this is what it means, but if you look carefully at James' words you will notice that he is not saying that you have to contort your feelings into enjoying the difficulties themselves. To do so would be dishonest and downright foolish—as if anyone in their right state of mind can enjoy pain or sadness. What you are called to do is to look beyond the trials to something else.

God is proving the authenticity of your faith

That something else is 'the testing of your faith' (v. 3) and the results it brings. I am not convinced that this way of putting it is the most helpful (nor in verse 12 where it appears as 'when he has stood the test'), even though it also appears in Genesis 22 where we are told that God tested Abraham (v. 1). Testing conjures up images of a teacher springing an unexpected exam on pupils to keep them on their toes, or a malicious dungeon-master who lays out a trail for intrepid adventurers that is laced with fiendish traps to fool the unwary and will see many of the party come to a nasty end. While 'testing' is probably a convenient way of describing what is happening, there is more happening than the English text suggests.

The word James uses means to prove someone's (or something's) worth. If you buy a piece of electrical equipment you will frequently find a small label attached bearing the word 'Tested'. This one word reassures you that the item has been checked over and will work. It is the genuine article and can be bought with confidence. Likewise, this concept here is not talking of a test to see if you are going to pass or fail, but of an event that demonstrates the reality and genuine nature of your faith. According to *Trench's Synonyms of the New Testament*, it is significant that this word is never used to describe the devil's testing of us, but only what God is doing.[2] The devil tests with a view to pulling down; God always brings circumstances into our lives that will prove that we are genuine.

> What you are called to do is to look beyond the trials to something else.

If you look at other instances of this word you will see this more clearly. The related noun appears in Romans 5:4 where Paul says that afflictions produce perseverance, which in turn produces *character*. That is, character that has been formed and refined by passing through trials. In this connection, the same noun is found in 1 Peter 1:7 to describe the reason behind the great suffering the Christians were enduring; it is translated as 'may be proved genuine'.

This changes my whole outlook on periods of difficulty. Viewing them as testing will induce an attitude that merely aims to hold on, perhaps resigned to the process, perhaps grimly determined, perhaps successful, but never joyful. However, knowing that these events are part of a process that proves my faith to be genuine indicates that there is a design (and a Designer) behind them. If only for this reason, I can welcome them with joy. But there is, of course, more than just this.

God matures your faith through this process

Putting it bluntly, this painful process gets results. James says that it produces 'perseverance' (v. 3), or the ability to hold on under pressure, to stand firm and not be drawn away from Christ. If you think about it, perseverance can by definition only be attained by sticking it out. You can't learn perseverance by pulling out early, much though you would probably like it that way. And God wants perseverance in the faith, since it marks out those who are his. Those who stand firm to the end are the ones who will be saved, so God engineers life in a way that will test and fortify the perseverance of the faithful. Perseverance, in its turn, has the effect of building character to create a well-rounded and complete individual in Christ. Look in James 1:3–4 at the way he describes the person who has gone through and persevered in trials.

This painful process gets results.

Such a person, he says, is 'mature', which is sometimes translated as 'perfect' in older versions, meaning that which is finished. Perseverance under difficult circumstances therefore finishes its work by bringing you to maturity, so that every grace in you is developed and whole, making you 'complete'. This second term has wholeness in mind, conveying the idea of someone who is sound in every part (in 1 Thessalonians 5:23 Paul uses it in a prayer that the entire person, body, soul and spirit, may be kept blameless), with the result that you 'lack nothing'.

Peter gives some insight into the way it happens in his first letter when he compares the trials we endure with the process of refining gold (1:7). The heat does not destroy the gold, but burns off the dross—that is the rubbish and impurities that may mix with the gold and debase it—and reveals the precious metal more clearly. We experience the same refining process: the heat of the trials we live through burns off the dross of our sinful nature and produces the gold of a mature and complete character that pleases God.

It is something of a paradox that this should be the outcome, since it seems to work so much against the normal run of events. God is aiming to produce Christians who are mature, consistent and strong in the faith, but such qualities do not naturally appear in his people. So how is he going to produce them? Most of us would like to think that it would be by giving us special pampering treatment, much like you might get on a visit to a health spa. A personal trainer guides you through a series of exercises that stretch you in a gentle, non-threatening manner, followed by lazy sessions on the sunbed or in the sauna to recuperate. That sounds wonderful. If only God could make me what he wants me to be that way. I could bask in the tranquil warmth of the sun and melt serenely into the shape God wants.

> God wants men and women with spiritual strength and backbone and the heat required to produce those qualities is far more intense, since the raw material is resistant and impure.

But you know that is not the way it happens. For a start, it is only jellies that melt so easily into any mould you want, but they don't keep their shape. They wobble when shaken and melt away again when the heat is turned back up. God wants men and women with spiritual strength and backbone and the heat required to produce those qualities is far more intense, since the raw material is resistant and impure. So he gives us his personal trainer, in the form of the Holy Spirit, who has radical refining, moulding and proving in mind and puts us into the searing heat of the furnace to achieve this.

Think of it all another way. We would like the process of growing to maturity to go like this:

Everything going well + prosperity + minimum effort = maturity.

Whereas James is describing a rather more difficult equation:

Trials + perseverance = maturity.

So what were your thoughts the last time you faced significant difficulties? That you should be rejoicing in trials? Probably not. In all likelihood you were wondering whether your faith would survive the pounding it was taking and were asking something along the lines of, 'Why is this happening? What is God doing? Is God doing *anything*?' When events take a nasty turn they seem pointless, random, out of control and with a fearful capacity to destroy you. Joy is not a natural or sensible reaction when you look at events from that angle.

But James is not looking from that angle. He is approaching the situation from the other side. We, rather like rabbits frozen in the glare of an approaching car's headlights, are blinded by what is bearing down on us. We become completely taken up with the events themselves, when we ought to be looking at what God is doing behind the scenes and be encouraged—no, rejoice—in that. God has a hand in your difficulties. They are not aimless, chance-driven events, nor are they purposeless disasters which God is watching helplessly, unable to offer assistance. James assures you that God has designed them for your strengthening in the faith and is standing with you in them. He is not aiming to bring you down. Of course, it will not feel like that in the heat of the flames—and the devil will be doing his level best at the same time to bring you down—but faith trusts that God knows what he is doing and has not left a friend in the lurch. It is only natural to look upon the trials of life as a threat, believing that bad events will be the cause of our downfall. Faith, however, sees that the very trial we fear will be the devil's instrument to destroy us is actually that which God has designed to make us stronger, and it rejoices in that fact.

> God knows what he is doing and has not left a friend in the lurch.

No one is pretending that this is going to be easy. The very fact that James says that you should pray for wisdom and not doubt (v. 5) tells us that he understands the emotional turmoil you can get into at such times. The wisdom he is thinking of is not the wisdom that has all the answers, but that which views current events in the light of this principle that God matures faith through adversity. It is the wisdom which therefore trusts God, holds on to him and does not accuse him of failure or doing wrong.

I have met people so shaken by what has happened to them that they cannot think straight about their faith. One moment they are apparently firm in their trust in God, the next it is as if God is to blame for everything and they question his love and his ability to direct their lives. They accuse God of putting obstacles in their path, of spitefully frustrating their plans and wishes, even tempting them to commit sin. It is as if he is trying to trick them into doing something they wouldn't do if they were in their right mind. Read the book of Job and you will see that Job faced an almost unbearable temptation to deny God in his suffering. It came from his wife. 'Curse God and die,' she advised, meaning, 'Why hold on to God when he has failed you (and me) so badly?' While Job rejected her suggestion, the record of his debates with his three friends reveals how deeply he was struggling with questions about God's purpose in his tragedies.

In this condition, you need God's wisdom, or you will inevitably be thrown around by doubt. God will bring something out of this time so that you will be stronger. Pure joy? Yes, most certainly! God is at work.

There is a reward to be obtained

Having said all this we must acknowledge that there is more to this than fortifying yourself with the knowledge that God is making your faith stronger. After all, there are circumstances in which you will not have much opportunity to grow further once the trial is over. Those martyred for their faith, for instance, were not motivated by the thought that they were growing in the faith as they faced execution. What enabled them to face sometimes horrible torture and death with joy was the certainty that they would soon be in the presence of the Lord and would receive their reward, that 'Well done!' from the Master's lips.

When Scottish Covenanter Donald Cargill faced his execution in Edinburgh on 27 July 1681, for no crime other than preaching in defiance of the king, he wrote a testimony in his cell during his last night that puts him among the line of those who understood what James was urging. One of the paragraphs begins: 'This is the most joyful day that I ever saw in my pilgrimage on earth. My joy is now begun which I see shall never be interrupted …' Later that day at the scaffold he paused to speak to the assembled crowds. He sang a psalm expressing his confidence that God was almighty, even in this situation, and assured them of his complete peace in Christ. 'I am no more terrified at death, nor afraid of hell, because of sin, than if I had never sinned; for all my sins are freely pardoned and washed away through the precious blood and intercession of Jesus Christ.' When he came to the foot of the ladder we are told that he 'blessed the Lord loudly with uplifted hands, that he was thus near the crown; and when setting foot upon the ladder to go up to embrace the bloody rope, he said, "The Lord knows I go up this ladder with less fear, confusion or perturbation of mind, than I ever entered a pulpit to preach."' Moments before he died he called out to his friends and urged them to 'set time apart and sing a song of praise to God, for what he has done to my soul, and my soul says, "To him be the praise."'3

In 1:12 James calls this reward 'the crown of life' that awaits those who persevere and whose faith is proved genuine. The crown of life is the victor's reward from God for those who have run the race and struggled to the end. It is a picture of the reward of heaven itself and is so great that it can only be described as 'life'. The trials we endure feel like the onset of death—and perhaps they are, in human terms. But from the angle of faith, they are the gateway to life. The reward God gives is the ultimate incentive to hold on in faith with joy. Whatever you lose through hanging on, you will not lose this.

Summary: God puts me through testing circumstances so that my faith may be proved genuine.

Key verse: James 1:2–3: 'Consider it pure joy … whenever you face trials of many kinds, because you know that the testing of your faith develops perseverance.'

To think about: How am I going to inject a note of joy into my current worries and troubles?

'Let us fix our eyes on Jesus, the author and perfecter of our faith, who for the joy set before him endured the cross, scorning its shame, and sat down at the right hand of the throne of God', Hebrews 12:2.

'Do not throw away your confidence; it will be richly rewarded. You need to persevere so that when you have done the will of God, you will receive what he has promised', Hebrews 10:35–36.

Thinking more deeply

Joy—the deep, sustaining joy that Jesus promises—is a gift from God that takes us by surprise.

Bill Hybels, *Losing to Win*

The command which Paul gives us in Philippians 3:1 acts as a bridge between what he has taught and what he is about to teach. Jesus has been glorified as God, Saviour, Example and Lord. So then *rejoice in the Lord.* He is about to be displayed as the Christian's pride, choicest possession, ambition, pattern, possessor, the crucified and coming Saviour. Should we not, then, *rejoice in the Lord*? The command may be understood better in the light of a similar phrase in 1:18. There Paul wrote, concerning the preaching of the gospel, 'in that I rejoice.' He meant, 'This is what brings joy to me'—this, and not that he should be well thought of by all, not that he should be released, and so forth. 'It is in this that I find my joy.' Similarly the command to *rejoice in the Lord* means 'Let the Lord alone be the one who makes you happy', 'Find your joy in him and in him alone.'

Alec Motyer, *Jesus our Joy: Commentary on Philippians.*

Notes

1 Quoted in **Jock Purves,** *Fair Sunshine: an account of the suffering of the Scottish Covenanters in the seventeenth century* (Edinburgh: The Banner of Truth Trust, 1968), p. 6.

2 **R.C. Trench,** *Trench's Synonyms of the New Testament* (London: James Clarke, 1961), p. 263.

3 An account of his execution can be found in **Purves,** *Fair Sunshine*, pp. 191–2.

2 Refining:
When your world collapses

God's higher aim in calamity

When we suffer, there will sometimes be mystery. Will there also be faith? (Don Carson, How long, O Lord?)

Please read Job 23.

A heavenly camera angle

The Frank Capra film *It's a Wonderful Life* begins from a heavenly viewpoint. People are praying for the lead character, played by Jimmy Stewart, who is at an all-time low and, since this is Hollywood, heaven answers by sending an angel who is a rather eccentric and scruffy character and needs some practice at doing his job. I'm not going to spoil it for you by telling you the ending of what is arguably one of the greatest feel-good films around, but suffice to say that this heavenly perspective at the beginning is needed to understand what the rest of the film is about. Without it, the film makes no sense at all.

The book of Job similarly begins with a heavenly viewpoint without which the rest of the book would be beyond comprehension. Rather than cutting straight to the action, it sets the scene. We meet the protagonists and read some important background notes about them and the events we are about to witness. It is important to realize that we are privileged to be able to read these notes, since they afford us a view on the unfolding drama that neither Job nor his friends are given. The disasters that sweep down on him and his family come without warning, so that he has to try to understand them unaided. If he had been able to read this prologue beforehand he would have looked at both the events and God's seeming absence in a different light, but of course he couldn't, and this is where the value of the story of Job lies. You and I do not get to read the director's notes before we are pitched into trials, either. Troubles arrive unannounced and often without explanation and we are left to fathom out what is going on ourselves. With Job's story, however, we are not completely in the dark.

The opening sentences of the book of Job paint a picture of both Job's prosperity and spirituality. Immensely rich, he was at the same time genuinely godly. It seems that people were as cynical 3000 years ago about rich believers as they can be now, finding it hard to accept that he could be sincere in his faith at the same time as possessing a vast fortune, but the writer insists that he was. Job possessed two qualities essential to true godliness in that he was both 'blameless and upright' (v. 1), having an inward purity alongside his outward integrity. Using the Old Testament shorthand term for belief in God, submission to him and a life of obedience, the writer tells us that Job 'feared God' and that he demonstrated this by the way that he 'shunned evil'. Note that this same series of terms appears two more times in these introductory chapters, spoken by God on those occasions, to confirm that this really is true of the man and that we should not doubt it even if everyone else appears to. The writer then cites one example of Job's authenticity in his faith. His concern for being right with God extended to the point of praying fervently that his children might also be pure, sacrificing offerings for them to cover unconfessed sin or sins against God that they might have only thought about.

The basic purpose of this introduction is to give us heaven's perspective on the man Job before we see him in debate with his friends. It tells us what God thinks of Job, which is a crucial piece of information to hold onto for a couple of reasons. Firstly, for much of the drama God is silent, so if we forget what he says at the beginning we will, like his friends, come to the wrong conclusions later—for instance that God is not pleased with Job. Secondly, the book loses its force and value if we are not certain that Job is a righteous man. If he is guilty of sin then his friends are right—he is being punished and should repent because he is a hypocrite. Moreover, the book's message becomes crassly simple: suffering is directly caused by your sin, so if you go through difficult times you should repent of anything and everything you can think of to restore God's blessing. But since we are told he is not guilty, while other difficult questions are raised, this book becomes a statement from God about the suffering of the righteous and a real source of strength.

After this brief introduction to the man, the picture moves to a heavenly scene in which angels are presenting themselves before the Lord when Satan turns up, rather like the thirteenth fairy in the Sleeping Beauty story. The Lord challenges him to consider 'my servant Job', a title reserved for only the most faithful followers of the Lord in the Old Testament, and his challenge is greeted with cynicism. Satan simply cannot believe that Job can be genuine since the Lord has protected him at every turn and has prospered everything he has done. Take all that away from him, Satan reasons, and he will reject faith altogether. It's a valid point. Religion can look very attractive if there are significant benefits attached to it, whether it provides a bowl of rice that keeps starvation at bay in India, curries favour with the factory bosses in Victorian England, guarantees heaven to martyrs, or just gives an aura of respectability that projects the right image to religious conservatives whose vote you need. These benefits, if they do not actually promote hypocrisy, do not make for a strong commitment to the faith. If removed, faith may simply evaporate like morning mist in the heat of the sun.

And so the test is born. Satan is given permission to take everything from Job in order to see what sort of faith he has. In one terrible day he takes all Job's children and possessions with a series of catastrophic body blows that leave him reeling. Yet his response is one of reverent submission to God, accepting that everything comes from God and that God is still Lord over his life and worthy of praise. Of course, when the Lord points this out to Satan at their next encounter, Satan is unimpressed. Once again he cynically accuses Job of acting out of pure self-interest, pointing out that Job lost possessions in the first attack, but was personally unscathed. If, however, Job himself was to suffer, the result would be different. So he receives the green light to afflict Job to within an inch of death and see what happens.

Before moving on I think we ought to pause to think about a couple of issues, the first of which is to consider the sticky question of just who is in control. Christians can be a little schizophrenic at this point out of a desire to protect God from unwarranted criticism (or themselves from questions they cannot answer), so they blame the devil for events like the ones Job endured, but they do so in such a way that gives the impression that the devil is the one calling the shots. Terms are used such as God 'allowing' these things to happen or 'giving permission' to the devil to attack us, but they are sometimes used so as to suggest that God had no other choice but to let the devil do this. The aim is a noble one, since it comes from a desire to avoid accusing God of wrongdoing, but it makes the mistake of giving the devil more power than he actually has, making him God's equal, and thus taking absolute control from God.

So let's get this straight. It is God who started all this. He is the one who challenged Satan first of all, pointing out what sort of a man Job was. He gave permission to Satan to test Job and take from him everything he held dear, and then defined the limits beyond which Satan could not go in his attacks. William Henry Green puts it even more strongly and says that Satan is 'actually exhibited in the attitude of a servant of God, and made subservient to the discipline and training of his people.'[1] And God is the one whom Job, without blaming him, named as responsible for these events, a responsibility which God accepted (notice that, at the end of the book, Satan does not feature and is not even mentioned). If you think about it, this is why disasters cause such a crisis of faith. If you believe that Satan has an element of control, then you really are in trouble and you will never have any peace of mind. But if God really loves and cares for us and is in control, then why does he bring such things into our lives? This is one of the oldest dilemmas for faith (and it is significant that the book of Job is one of the oldest pieces in the Bible, indicating that true faith has never ducked the issue), but we are not going to solve it by pushing God into the background.

One of the most influential books on suffering is *When Bad Things Happen to Good People*. Written by a rabbi, Harold Kushner, after the tragic death of his son, it explores the difficult questions posed by suffering and tragedy, particularly in the lives of the innocent (evangelical Christians can be rather cynical at this point, observing correctly that no one is sinless or absolutely innocent and that the real surprise is that so much good happens to bad people. But that is to miss the point of the book of Job, where we are deliberately told on several occasions, that Job was upright and pleasing to God). Although Kushner is a Jew and has this book of Job at his disposal he rejects the traditional view and concludes that God could not have prevented his son's death. He finds it impossible to accept that God could bring suffering into the lives of the innocent, so he is forced into the conclusion that God was not able to help. And that, of course, is the problem. If God is not in control, then some other being is (or is at least of equal power to God and able to thwart him) and we end up with a god who cannot give comfort other than sitting alongside us and wringing his hands with us, and who is equally unable to help.

A second observation about these introductory chapters is that they confirm that we are right in our understanding of what James says of the nature of testing. This is not some arbitrary or cruel experiment that is designed to catch Job out and watch him suffer and fail. It starts on the assumption that he will succeed, that his faith will be proved genuine. God is so convinced that Job's faith is genuine that he holds it up before the angelic world, an audience which includes the greatest sceptic of them all, and announces that he is pleased with Job. It is almost as if, like some travelling circus ringmaster, he is showing off his champion and inviting all comers to feel his muscles, square up to him and go three rounds with him in the ring.

> God is so convinced that Job's faith is genuine that he holds it up before the angelic world, an audience which includes the greatest sceptic of them all, and announces that he is pleased with Job.

Evangelical Christians in particular can be so conscious of personal sinfulness that we find this notion of God's satisfaction with his people difficult to accept. Rightly acknowledging that sin taints and twists every part of human nature, we then wrongly conclude that it is impossible that anything we do will really please God and so the difficulties we face are in some way deserved—we are being punished in some way, or there is something we need to repent of, a hidden sin that has got to be confessed, a lesson that God needs to teach us. What this does is that it makes the trial perhaps easier to understand (if there is something wrong with us then there is an explanation for it), but it only achieves this by making a wrong assumption that in fact dishonours God and the person experiencing the difficulties.

When I was a student pastor in the north-west of England I encountered a man—a strong believer—who was dying of cancer. Not surprisingly his faith had been stretched and squeezed by his illness, but the greatest test had come from assumptions and accusations made by other Christians about his faith and the reason why this was happening to him. One particularly zealous—and pretty heartless—couple had insisted on praying over him for his healing and had then blamed his lack of faith when it had not taken place. More than this, rather like Job's friends we will meet in a moment, they had stated that there must have been some unconfessed sin in his life, both to cause the illness in the first place and now to account for his continuing failure to be healed. I didn't meet the couple in question, nor the church they were attached to which had this emphasis, but it seems that their belief system could not cope with the dilemma of unanswered prayer and the suffering of a righteous person. Threatened by the apparent failure of God, they found it easier to blame the man, because the only other alternative seemed to be to blame God (it certainly wouldn't have occurred to them to blame themselves), but if Job has anything to teach us it is that the man needn't have been at fault at all, and that God might not have wanted to heal him.

That is a hard conclusion to come to because it leaves so many other questions unanswered, and yet they are just the sort of issues that the book addresses. The suffering of the innocent has no easy answers, much though people try to give them.

Who needs enemies?

That leads us to the subject of Job's friends who came to sympathize with him in his loss. The term 'Job's comforters' has entered our language as a byword for the sort of insensitive, open-your-mouth-and-put-your-foot-in-it people who mean well but make you wish the New Testament writer James had recommended a good slapping for those who cannot keep control of their tongues. Yet Job's friends were not village gossips who had come looking for fresh tittle-tattle. Their reaction when they first saw him indicates they were real friends. Read their speeches and you will see that they were deep thinkers about God, devout and sincere, probably respected community leaders like Job. But the spectacle of Job sitting on the ruins of his life protesting his innocence, even though all the evidence appeared to point to divine judgement as the cause of his calamities, was too much for them. It just didn't fit their preconceived theological ideas—come to think of it, it didn't fit with Job's either, but the difference was that he was experiencing the dilemma first-hand while knowing he was innocent—and so the only conclusion they could arrive at was that Job was a hypocrite.

They started off well. It took them a week to recover from the shock of seeing the wreckage of the successful man they once knew now on the ash-heap, during which time they simply sat with him, saying nothing. Pop star Ronan Keating once produced a song that extolled the virtues of non-verbal communication between lovers that contained the words, 'You say it best when you say nothing at all.' Hardly deep stuff there from one of Ireland's favourite sons, but Job's friends prove that it applies equally (if not more so) to the matter of sympathizing with sufferers. There are times when trauma is so deep that nothing we can say will provide a satisfactory answer, and speaking will only make matters worse. Job's friends' silent comfort and sympathy was the best thing they did for him. If only they could have kept it up.

> There are times when trauma is so deep that nothing we can say will provide a satisfactory answer.

I suppose they expected that Job should pour his heart out to them. After all, they had come to help him and had gained his trust by sitting with him for a week without judging him or attempting to provide answers, but it was the nature of his complaint that took them all by surprise. Job's initial wail of despair (Job 3), wishing that he had never been born, sounded like he was raging against God. It seems something clicked at that point in their heads and they sprang to God's defence, in a restrained manner at first, but with increasing animosity and dogmatism in the face of Job's continued insistence that he had done nothing to deserve this.

It is hard to say exactly what they were expecting from their arguments with Job, but their speeches betray a belief about God that suggests to me they were looking for a statement of repentance or even a detailed confession of sin. Their beliefs about God were thoroughly orthodox and not to be faulted: God is completely just and fair; he judges sin and evildoers; he rewards righteous, moral, virtuous behaviour; he punishes sin. It was their application of these principles to the experience of Job that was the problem. He had previously given every appearance of being a good, God-fearing man and they felt he had the riches to prove he had God's blessing. But all of a sudden everything was taken from him, so what were they to conclude? God could not be so unjust as to let a righteous man suffer in this way, so it must be the case that Job had been a hypocrite all along and he had now been unmasked. In their minds there could be no other explanation for these events.

The suffering of the innocent has always caused problems of this nature to both sufferers and observers. You know it yourself because certain questions always spring to mind: 'What have I done to deserve this? Is God trying to get even? Am I being punished for something I did?' It even appears in pop music. 'Why does it always rain on me?' is a question posed by the pop group Travis in their best-selling single: 'Is it because I lied when I was seventeen?' We laugh at their attempts at finding an answer, knowing there is no connection between those two things, but the basic notion is not so easy to shake off. Bad things happen because we must have done something bad. All Job's friends are doing is looking at him in the light of this principle.

Eliphaz, the first, and probably most senior, of his friends to speak, hints at this within a few moments of beginning his first response to Job's outburst (Job 4–5). He chides Job gently, 'Surely you should have confidence before God that your previous committed faith will stand you in good stead before him? You shouldn't be afraid, because the innocent don't perish …'—and I wince at the way he says 'As I have observed' (4:8), which comes across rather like 'in my humble opinion'—' … and trouble only comes to those who sow evil in their lives.' With these words he effectively sets the tone for the rest of the debate by insinuating that Job is being punished in some way for sin, or disciplined and corrected, as he says towards the end of his speech. Like the other two friends, Eliphaz's theologically correct mindset has painted him into a corner: God cannot be unjust, so Job must have done something wrong. His resulting conclusion is the rather arrogant suggestion that Job should appeal to God for help because he rescues and prospers those who come to him.

I imagine that Job listened to Eliphaz with growing disbelief. Instead of supporting and comforting his friend, Eliphaz is lecturing him as if he was a schoolboy whose guilt he suspects but cannot prove and so he is laying it on thick to put the pressure on him. He is speaking with all the authority of a headmaster who is using every ounce of moral superiority to extract a confession and bringing what he believes to be his superior experience and wisdom to bear on the situation. But his advice shows that he has just not understood either Job or God and what he says is an insult to both. Job was suffering, but innocent; the whole basis of his life up to that point had been to honour God and seek his blessing in everything he did; and God was not punishing Job. Eliphaz has nothing to say of any real help to Job, but there is much worse to come.

Bildad leaps in with both feet (Job 8), accusing Job of slandering God, and stating that Job's children got what they deserved when they sinned against God. Zophar (Job 11) says that God has even forgotten some of Job's sins, implying that Job has so many that God could have made things even worse if he had taken all his sins into account. Then Eliphaz, evidently stung by Job's dogged refusal to admit his guilt, returns to the fray (Job 15) and starts a theme which the others take up when he gives a detailed description of the fate of the wicked, threatening Job with the most dire punishments for sins if he will not admit them. When he speaks for a third time (Job 22) Eliphaz goes so far as detailing Job's alleged evils and says that basically Job is a first-class hypocrite who performed religious duties but exploited other people.

So where did all that come from? We witness three men savage a close friend more ferociously than any minister resigning in protest from government would experience, hounding him for a confession with all the determination of the Spanish Inquisition and badgering him with unparalleled insensitivity to his grief. Any neutral observer would be asking what is going on. What has Job done to merit such treatment from his friends—who have lost nothing themselves, nor been attacked by him—when all he has done is lose everything he ever had? The answer must lie in the fact that Job is not the only person whose world has fallen apart.

When terrorists flew passenger planes into the Twin Towers of the World Trade Center on 11th September 2001 one remark was made more than any other: that the world would never be the same. This overworked phrase also says something about the effect of disaster in the book of Job. The four friends had previously inhabited a cosy world where they knew certain truths would always apply. God would always bless the righteous and punish the wicked, so that people would always reap what they sowed. The righteous would prosper, while the wicked would both fail in this life and also face God's judgement. Simple—at least until Job went down in flames, and then their entire worldview went down with him. With the demise of a good man who had been faithful to God, suddenly nothing was certain and nothing would ever be the same. What about God punishing evil? Or the righteous always being blessed? How does Job now fit this law of cause and effect? They have no answers other than trying to shore up their crumbling belief system by accusing Job of crimes he did not commit. Their debates with Job, therefore, are the rearguard action of a worldview that is dying because it does not fit reality and God has to tell them at the end that they have not spoken wisely. They were wrong.

The long and short of it is that other people feel threatened by catastrophe because an earthquake that rocks you to the foundations will shake them, too. Their belief systems can be undermined by such events because they don't fit what they have previously understood about life or God. But because they are only experiencing these things second-hand they can push them away and not think about them too hard, which means that they may push you away at the same time. Job's friends end up pushing him away because he won't admit that it is all his fault. An over-zealous couple insult a dying man and question his faith because they cannot believe that God does not heal unless something is blocking the power. But they are not the only ones. Sufferers, whether cancer patients, people who lose children in tragic circumstances, or those going through divorce, all relate that they see once good friends cross the road to avoid having to talk to them. 'What would I say?' is one of the reasons usually given for such behaviour. Frequently these people are afraid of not having answers to that awful question 'Why?'. Maybe they just don't want to say the wrong thing; they don't think that God is punishing you, but they don't know what he is doing, either, so the effect is very similar: they shun their friends at the time their friends most need them.

The phenomenal success of the TV series *Friends* comes at least in part from its portrayal of real supporting companionship for a generation weighed down with emotional baggage from its parents' divorces and general family collapse. It is interesting that the parents of the six main characters always appear in a negative light and offer no real support, but the friends affirm each other, stick together and come through for each other in the end. Ross and Rachel, for instance, do things that would destroy each other in the real world—fall in and out of love (and bed) several times, misunderstand and insult one another frequently, form other relationships out of spite, get married in Las Vegas while drunk and then have the marriage annulled—but they still finish up arm in arm. Sadly, relationships in the real world—even Christian ones—cannot take such a battering and, much though we would like it to be different, we know that major crises can stretch friendships to breaking point. But if friends fail us, then at least we have God. Don't we?

> Even God seems to have deserted him.

The sound of silence

You don't need a degree in psychoanalysis to see that Job does not feel like the champion mentioned earlier. True enough, he defends himself vigorously against his friends' withering assault on his integrity and eventually argues them into the ground, but he gains no satisfaction from winning the debate. His friends were his last source of comfort in the world, so now he has lost everything. He is completely alone. Even God seems to have deserted him.

The title of a book by Philip Yancey, *Where is God when it hurts?*, says everything about Job's condition. 'He is not there … I do not find him … I do not see him … I catch no glimpse of him' are what he has to say in 23:8–9 in response to a recommendation from Eliphaz that he submit to God and be at peace with him. Since this is not the only occasion on which Job laments God's silence and apparent absence, it is undoubtedly the most painful part of the trial he is facing. Psalm 139 speaks about David's sense of amazement and wonder that God is everywhere, that there is nowhere he can go where God is not already present, but Job's complaint is that he wishes this were true for him. If he could only know where God was, hear his voice and sense his approval once more, all the rest would be more bearable. Indeed, when God finally appears at the end of the book, Job is silent because his desires have been answered: God has returned and that is enough. In the meantime, however, he must labour on alone.

From a pastoral point of view the silence of God is one of the most difficult issues to handle, because it is among the most difficult to endure. Facing illness, for example, without a sense of God being near can be hellish. I knew of a Christian woman who was so embittered by her illness and her anger that God should abandon her to a slow death that she could not even bear to see the Bible in the minister's hand and ruled prayer at the bedside out of the question. Back at home we prayed for her and simply asked that God would give her his peace, which he did. Not long afterwards she took Communion once again, shortly after which she slipped away peacefully.

For those who have never experienced this sense of abandonment it is difficult to describe what is going on. To the sceptic looking on, it appears so subjective and introspective, but it is very real. The sense of losing God's smile when trouble strikes is rather like a tsunami that washes repeatedly over the shore in a series of devastating waves. Disaster strikes, but is then followed by a series of frightening emotions and questions, each with the potential to swamp the sufferer completely. Some form of disbelief or even denial is usually the first—'This can't be happening to me', is one expression of it, followed by 'God will get me out of this soon.' My own observation is that if people go through this phase they are often able to express their faith in God quite strongly at first, as if there is some kind of spiritual adrenaline flowing through the veins, but they are not able to keep it up for very long. Joni Eareckson Tada recounts that when she broke her neck in a diving accident she tried to witness to the nursing staff who were attending her in the emergency room, telling them she was confident that God would heal her. Her faith was genuine, but she was probably also not aware of the real seriousness of her condition, so when reality dawned that she would never walk again she felt quite differently.[2] Job's initial reaction was exemplary: when he mourned the loss of his children we are told that he worshipped God as he did so, but this quiet acceptance of his circumstances did not last.

After a week of silent sympathy from his friends Job's anger bubbled over (Job 3), not because they had said the wrong thing (that would come later), but because they had gained his trust by sitting with him in silence and he evidently thought they would understand how he felt. His sense of loss is so deep that he curses the day he was born, essentially wishing he was dead. Later speeches reveal a simmering resentment at the unfairness of it all, that he has done nothing to deserve this (look at 23:11, where he states truthfully that he had not departed from God's ways) and that God, who appears to be punishing him but not the wicked, is conveniently out of reach and will not answer for what he has done.

Anger at God is one of the most frightening emotions to surface at such times. It seems so wrong that a believer should be reduced to this, because raging against God is one of the more obvious attributes of unbelief. Christians fear that, by expressing it, they are on the slippery slope to apostasy, and so do everything to pretend that they are at peace with God even if they are not happy with their circumstances. Underneath, however, they are seething that God has put them in this mess, that he has brought such trouble into their lives (or merely allowed it, but the result is the same) and that he has failed to help them when they have remained faithful to him; surely he ought to be punishing the hooligans round the corner who beat up old ladies rather than persecuting someone who has always endeavoured to keep a clear conscience in everything. Naturally they don't express it this way—perhaps they don't even admit it to themselves—for fear of insulting God by questioning his ways and being thought a heretic by their friends, so they suppress their feelings and wind up resenting both God and their friends instead. By contrast, Job had no hesitation in letting people know his anger and, while he had to endure the censure of his friends, nevertheless found God's approval. Francis Andersen notes that this 'silences the cant of those who remind us of the inscrutability of God, and smugly say, "It is not for us to question the ways of the Almighty!" For that is precisely what Job does, and God says that he was fully justified in doing so. The Lord welcomes this exercise in moral judgement from man's side, even when it is directed in judgement on God himself!'[3]

Anger is not the last of the tidal waves to wash over us, for it frequently settles down into depression and resignation. These are not so immediately destructive, but take the form of a defeated and despairing outlook that cripples confident faith because it sees only bleakness and futility. 'Disaster has struck and God has left me to fend for myself. He did nothing to prevent it happening and has nothing to say about it now. I therefore have no answers and, because God is silent, I will have none in future.' People in this condition are often spiritually exhausted and lethargic, possessing neither the courage nor the will to change. There is more than a little of this in Job's rambling thoughts as he laments that God has abandoned him and no longer speaks to him, and yet it is in this desolate misery that God does communicate something to him. Even before the great revelation at the end, when God appears and silences everyone, something breaks through to Job's mind quite suddenly.

A glimmer of hope

Being a child of the 1960s I grew up with the twice weekly diet of the popular children's TV programme *Blue Peter*. Monday and Thursday evenings after school Britain's most famous trio of presenters, Valerie Singleton, John Noakes and Peter Purves, treated us to model-making, cooking, stories, music, animal antics, and expeditions into the wider world. One of these episodes has remained with me more than others, perhaps because experience has taught me that it reflects life more closely than the programme makers could have foreseen. The broadcast in question was the report of a day on a horse-drawn canal boat, a gentle excursion into a bygone age—gentle, that is, until the route inevitably led to a tunnel. Modern canal boats are not hindered by tunnels because they have their own engines, but a horse-drawn boat will find itself without power in such circumstances because the towpath does not run through the tunnel. This meant that Valerie had to lead the horse over the top, while the other two had to lie on the roof of the canal boat, place their feet firmly on the tunnel roof and propel the craft along a mile or so of tunnel with their feet, 'walking' the boat to the other end.

If you have walked down a tunnel you will know that the darkness envelops you with astonishing rapidity. You only need go down the tunnel twenty or thirty yards and you cannot see anything in front of you. The light behind you quickly recedes almost to nothing and ahead becomes so dark that, as the saying goes, you cannot see your hand in front of your face. So while Val walked in the sunshine above, John and Peter sweated and laboured to take the boat along the tunnel in almost absolute blackness. If it was not absolute it was because, once every quarter of a mile or so, there was a ventilation shaft cut down through the hillside to the tunnel roof. From underneath, it showed a distant patch of sky and cast a gloomy light onto the boat as it passed under, bringing a faint reminder of the sunshine outside. But it was only brief. The boat drifted slowly under its pale glow (it could hardly be called a beam), into the light for a few seconds, and then glided back into the shadows once more.

I cannot think of anything that more accurately describes Job's experience than this. His life has moved from the sunshine of God's presence and blessing to a seemingly God-forsaken tunnel of disaster with shocking speed. When we meet him in Job 23 he is truly in the dark and there is no light at the end of the tunnel, so for much of the time he is groping for answers. But every so often something shines through from above and illuminates his mind, cooling his anger and melting his despair. If only for a split second he sees clearly as he passes under the Spirit's beam. His frantic debating and desperate searching pause briefly as he suddenly understands something about his circumstances with a spiritual clarity that his friends never attain. But it is only for a moment and shortly afterwards he drifts back into the darkness once more. Job 23:10 is such a moment.

Reassuring clarity

The clarity with which Job sees what is going on in this verse is quite striking and means that he must in some way have had a glimpse of the heavenly scene that the book begins with. It is not enough to give him perfect peace, since he can't see everything, but what he does see is right. Beautifully simple, this verse has profound insight into the way God works through trials and stands as a light in his darkness that shines for us, too.

HE KNOWS THE WAY I TAKE ...

Job's friends have assumed that God is punishing him and Job knows they are wrong, but the only evidence he has is that God appears to have abandoned him, which is not much better. He is terribly alone and yearns for God's reassurance and cannot find it. Yet this short phrase indicates that Job has seen that he is not like a lost child, separated from his parents in the crowd. God is not ignoring him, but is fully aware of his circumstances.

Reassuring (and true) though this is, it may not in fact be the best translation of this verse, which could instead read 'He knows his way with me'. Put this way it is a statement of faith from Job, not merely that God knows where he is, but that these events are God-driven. It is possible to have a view of God that puts him in the background: he is aware of what is happening, but not involved, either because he is powerless to help or because he doesn't want to. What Job states indicates that God is intimately wrapped up in everything that happens to us to the point that he is the one who determines what is going on, and Job is content that this is so. He is happy to let God have his way.

> God is intimately wrapped up in everything that happens to us to the point that he is the one who determines what is going on.

I recall listening to British actor Stewart Granger speak about his life in an interview on radio. He was a swashbuckling hero in films of the late 1940s onwards—*The Prisoner of Zenda*, for instance—always dashing, with aristocratic bearing and a suave hint of grey in his swept-back hair. As with so many actors a successful career was mirrored by failures in marriage, so that there seemed to be one broken relationship after another. At the end of the programme he was invited to choose his favourite song and significantly he came up with Frank Sinatra's rendering of 'My Way'. An anthem to self-achievement, this very popular song could not have been more apt. He chose it because for him it expressed the guiding principles of his life—rugged self-determination, true grit, individuality and so on—but I felt that he was unwittingly describing the cause of the wreckage he had left in his wake. He had done it all his way and the results were plain to see. It changed my view of both the actor and the song and made me realize that doing things my way is a short cut to calamity.

God's way is what you need, even if God's way is not what you would choose. Even though Job cannot find God, he has evidently come round to a certain acceptance of the circumstances God has placed upon him, and you and I face the same struggle. His flash of inspiration here indicates that he can see that God is having his way and, painful though it is at the moment while it leads through terrain he would naturally avoid, it is nevertheless God's way. He would not admit to being happy with the way things are, but he is at peace with God in them. Perhaps more than anything else, it is vital that you come to the same point.

WHEN HE HAS TESTED ME I SHALL COME FORTH AS GOLD

The ability to arrive at peace with God about difficult circumstances will be strengthened by the knowledge that God is doing something through them.

> God's way is what you need, even if God's way is not what you would choose.

The events that have overwhelmed Job are God's means of testing and proving his faith, and in James 1 we saw that this testing produces character, but Job puts it in a more poetic term—gold. The gold that he envisages is, as in James, that of mature character in Christ, achieved through a painful refining and purification process. The dross of my life will be burned off so that the gold remains and shines out, an image which Peter also uses in his first letter.

It is a remarkable breakthrough for Job to arrive at this conclusion, as it is for anyone in such circumstances. Job's friends have made an entirely natural assumption for devout believers that his life is a wreck because God is punishing him; today, most people with a secular mindset would suppose that fate had been unkind or that he had been the victim of a piece of cosmic bad luck. But, quite astonishingly, Job has seen otherwise. Through the pain and darkness he has been able to see the hand of God in everything that has happened to him up to this point and at the same time has glimpsed a future outcome that his friends cannot imagine.

The best person to comment on whether this refining process is real or not is someone who has experienced it directly herself. While not an exact parallel with Job because she feels that her life needed some changing, Joni Eareckson Tada's reflection on her own paralysis from her diving accident is still extremely helpful:

In the psalms we're told that God does not deal with us according to our sins and iniquities. My accident was not a punishment for my wrongdoing—whether or not I deserved it. Only God knows why I was paralysed. Maybe he knew I'd be happier serving him. If I were still on my feet, it's hard to say how things might have gone. I probably would have drifted through life—marriage, maybe even divorce—dissatisfied and disillusioned. When I was in high school, I reacted to life selfishly and never built on any long-lasting values. I lived simply for each day and the pleasure I wanted—and almost always at the expense of others.

I wouldn't change my life for anything. I even feel privileged. God doesn't give such special attention to everyone and intervene that way in their lives. He allows most people to go right on in their own ways. He doesn't interfere even though he knows they are ultimately destroying their lives, health or happiness, and it must grieve him terribly. I am really thankful that he did something to get my attention and change me.[4]

God's way is far from easy, but a heavenly panorama reveals that he has an aim in mind that nothing else can reach: pure gold.

Summary: God knows the way he is taking me.

Key verse: Job 23:10: 'But he knows the way that I take; when he has tested me, I shall come forth as gold.'

To think about: How does it help me to know that God is leading me through the darkness? Look back over difficult times in the past as well as applying this to current testing times.

'These [trials] have come so that your faith—of greater worth than gold, which perishes even though refined by fire—may be proved genuine and may result in praise, glory and honour when Jesus Christ is revealed', 1 Peter 1:7.

'You have taken my companions and loved ones from me; the darkness is my closest friend', Psalm 88:18.

Thinking more deeply

Leaders being refined: Pete Greig is one of the leaders of the 24–7 prayer movement that has sprung up among young people worldwide. With his wife Samie's illness, his whole perspective changed:

All this has had a profound effect on us personally and, I think, on the 24–7 movement. At a time when we might have become triumphalistic and trite, intoxicated with the excitement of miracles and movements, we were suddenly confronted with the stark reality of suffering, unanswered prayer and even death. Samie and I were beginning to understand Paul's experience of a 'thorn in the flesh', allowed by God to keep him from 'becoming conceited' because of his incredible experiences. Like him, we plead with God to take our suffering away, and yet in the midst of it all we have discovered that his promises are true: 'My grace is sufficient for you for my power is made perfect in weakness' (2 Corinthians 12:9).

Of course, Samie and I are not the only ones to suffer. Many of the key leaders within 24–7 have found themselves struggling with enormous difficulties too. Some have been bereaved, one guy's wife walked out on him, triggering a nervous breakdown, another found her diabetes getting steadily worse, many face real financial challenges as they seek to follow the call on their lives. Whatever the 'thorn', these things keep us feeling weak, dependent on God and painfully aware that all the amazing stuff we've experienced as a movement is entirely thanks to him. 'Therefore,' Paul continues, 'I will boast all the more gladly about my weaknesses, so that Christ's power may rest on me … For when I am weak, then I am strong' (2 Corinthians 12:9–10).

Pete Greig, *Red Moon Rising*.

Think of [yourselves] as both musicians needing constant practice and work and as instruments needing mellowing and refining through years of being made and used. See [yourselves] as being prepared for some magnificent 'symphony' under the Conductor's direction, facing what is ahead of us in his plan for eternity. We are to be handmade instruments and also diligent music students, preparing and being prepared for a concert ahead, in which the preparation time has significance—*really* matters. Our today has a reality of meaning beyond the present. The refining and preparation have a day of fulfilment ahead.

Edith Schaeffer, *Affliction*.

Notes

1 **William Henry Green,** *Conflict and Triumph: The Argument of the Book of Job Unfolded* (Edinburgh: The Banner of Truth Trust, 1999), p. 21.

2 **Joni Eareckson,** *Joni* (London: Pickering and Inglis, 1978).

3 **Francis Andersen,** *Job* (Tyndale Old Testament Commentary series; Leicester: IVP, 1977), p. 66.

4 **Eareckson,** *Joni*, p. 206.

3 Obedience:
Pushed to the limit

Complete surrender

Here Abraham's faith looms up as positively heroic (H.C. Leupold, Exposition of Genesis).

Please read Genesis 22.

I have heard it said that you don't know whether you are really obeying God or just following your own ideas until he crosses your path and asks you to do something you don't want to do, and I think the point is well made. How do you know you are not merely pleasing yourself when everything is going your way? It is quite easy to say you are following Jesus Christ while his commands fit in with what you find acceptable or do not obstruct your own plans, but what will happen if he tells you to modify your cherished schemes and go down a route you do not like or surrender something you do not wish to give? Business partnerships can founder on disagreements like this and friendships fail, but what is going to happen if God signals his disagreement with the way you are going and requests a change of direction?

> How do you know you are not merely pleasing yourself when everything is going your way?

Nothing prepared Abraham for the shock of the complete change of direction that God requested, which came without warning and without explanation, reversing everything that had been achieved since Abraham had left his native country more than thirty years previously. There were no clouds in his relationship with God so it would have dropped on him out of a clear sky: sacrifice Isaac.

For all its difficulty and unexpectedness, this test is nevertheless the last in a long line of testing circumstances that Abraham had faced. It is, of course, the most severe, but there is a sense in which the whole of Abraham's life had been building up to this point. When he left his native city of Ur in Chaldea, he did so on the basis of an instruction from God that he should go and head for a land God would show him. Now towards the end of his life of faith he is faced with a command to go on another journey and sacrifice his son Isaac on a mountain God will show him. Both incidents required faith and between them lay a life of growing faith in which he learned progressively to trust God for everything: he believed God would look after his material well-being when he left Ur in the first place; in a quarrel with Lot he learned to trust God to give him the best inheritance; in war he trusted God to protect him and give victory; in prayer for the city of Sodom he learned to speak boldly with God; and then he learned to wait for God to fulfil his promise to give him and Sarah a son, Isaac. Now at the culmination of his life of faith, Abraham, known in Scripture as the man of faith, is pushed to the limit.

> Each test brought him closer to God.

Denis Lane has a significant comment about Abraham's life of growing faith. He observes that we may be tempted to feel sorry for Abraham, because we are reading this summary of his life as if it were a catalogue of disasters and mishaps, one thing after another that took things away from him and demands that God kept placing on him. But that is to fail to see that each test brought him closer to God. Time and again he was forced to act in trust that God would support him, each time that trust was vindicated, and this occasion would be no different. To follow God is to be taken deeper and deeper into a relationship with him that calls for trust that grows step by step. Lane comments, 'To people today, Christianity means living exactly as we did before, but with joy and peace in our hearts, a smooth path ahead and heaven at the end. The radical nature of the change that a living trust in the crucified Lord brings has not dawned on them. They have never known a situation where they are cast wholly upon God and nothing else, and therefore they have never known the joy of proving him to be there and the growth in faith that such an experience provides.'[1] That radical change is what we have in view here.

'Why do you call me "Lord, Lord" but do not do what I say?'

There are several points at which Abraham is being tested—for instance, does he believe God knows what he is doing? Is there anything that Abraham is withholding from God? What (and who) is most important to him? and so on—but they all revolve around whether he is going to do what God says. Obedience lies at the heart of faith, not merely because obedience follows faith, but because the faith we exercise is itself sometimes referred to as obedience. For instance, in Romans 15:18 Paul talks of his own work as a missionary in terms of 'leading the Gentiles to obey God', while Peter in his first letter looks at those on the other side of the divide and describes those who do not believe as 'those who do not obey the gospel of God' (1 Peter 4:17). The very act of believing is an exercise of obedience to God in which we finally heed his call to surrender, stop fighting against him, admit that we are sinners, accept his offer of free pardon and put our faith in his Son, the Lord Jesus Christ. Not believing, by definition, continues the disobedience that separates us from him.

> The testing of obedience has always been a natural part of human relationships with God.

Of course, obedience also follows faith and is a natural and inseparable partner to it. We are, according to Paul, 'slaves … to obedience' because we have offered ourselves to God (Romans 6:16) and because in the gospel God calls us 'to the obedience that comes from faith' (Romans 1:5). Jesus makes the same basic link between these two elements. 'Whoever has my commands and obeys them, he is the one who loves me … If anyone loves me, he will obey my teaching' (John 14:21,23). The equation is quite simple: Any claim you might make to love Jesus can only be regarded as genuine if you also do what he says.

For this reason, the testing of obedience has always been a natural part of human relationships with God. The very first test of obedience comes very early in the Bible, when Adam and Eve are placed in the garden and given free rein. They can do anything they like, except eat from the fruit of the tree of the knowledge of good and evil. Just one rule, no experience of sin and a completely harmonious relationship with God to strengthen them in their resolve to keep it, yet they still manage to break it. There are plenty of questions that arise from that incident which we cannot think about here, yet we can say that the purpose of the command's existence was to test Adam and Eve's obedience. God wants willing, joyful obedience from his people and that one command embodied in the tree's presence in the garden gave him his answer. We live with Adam and Eve's legacy today: give children boundaries and you can be certain that they will push them to the limit and step over them.

Since we are not sinless we are not in the same position as Adam and Eve, but the testing of obedience is nevertheless an essential ingredient in the maturing of faith. It brings the equation mentioned earlier (love leads to obedience) into sharper focus and forces the believer to demonstrate faith in action, but it may also reveal whether faith is genuine or not. In Luke's account of the Parable of the Sower, seed is scattered on rocky places where it grows quickly, but then withers away in the heat of the day. Jesus says that this refers to 'those … who receive the word with joy when they hear it, but [who] have no root. They believe for a while, but in the time of testing they fall away' (Luke 8:13). He does not specify what this time of testing could be—both James and Job have given us some idea—but it could simply refer to a test of obedience in which God asks them to do something and they refuse. I have seen it happen in the way Jesus describes it. An initial declaration of faith is followed by a burst of enthusiasm, but shortly afterwards faith shrivels and fades. It may be nothing more than unfamiliar difficulties that show up the true cost of following Jesus—in other words, the cost of obedience—in a clearer light, but the effect is sadly familiar: faith which initially looks to be well-grounded and productive is shown to be without root and empty.

Most pastors and youth leaders will tell you that they see this issue of obedience played out most frequently in the area of male and female relationships, particularly (although not exclusively) among the youth element of the church. In any church youth group the question of whether a Christian should go out with or marry a non-Christian will be among the top three headaches (and heartaches) as young Christians wrestle with what it means to follow Jesus. Keen to honour him and only have a Christian partner, most will nevertheless have problems in this area, if only because of a shortage of eligible members of the opposite sex in the church they attend. The notion of singleness can conjure up images of a frantic Bridget Jones, desperately hoping for the man of her dreams to come her way, and some are thereby tempted to throw themselves at the first candidate they meet, suitable or otherwise. This sets up one of the most common trials of strength between God and those who claim to be his disciples: Will they respect God's command about marriage—unambiguously and frequently expressed in Scripture—or will they settle for something less? Those who opt for the less costly route usually find that this compromise undermines faith in the long-term. Having failed to obey one of God's clearer commands, they drift slowly away from deeper commitment. Many never come back. Yet those who take the painful (I use the word advisedly) option by putting God's wishes ahead of their own prove their commitment to him and emerge stronger for the experience.

In my own case this was the first way in my Christian life in which my faith and obedience were seriously tested. I met a young woman who was not a Christian about four months after I became a Christian and we started going out. When it came to reading the Bible I had not yet worked my way right through the whole book, so there were plenty of passages that were still new to me, and it was around that period that I encountered 2 Corinthians 6:14–18 for the first time. The passage does not mention marriage specifically, but the import of what it was saying was obvious—what would we have in common?—and struck me so forcefully that I knew I had to finish the relationship before it got too serious. I also realized at the time that this was a matter of basic discipleship—was I going to obey God, or just go my own way and effectively lock him out of one area of my life? Difficult as it was to do, I wrote a letter and said goodbye.

A place where God cannot go?
It feels impertinent of me to compare myself with Abraham and the test he faced. Ending a relationship is hardly on the same level as being asked to end a life, but the nature of the command from God was the same in both

cases in that it demanded that God be given access to private life and that a vital part of it be surrendered to him.

The Bible's concept of obedience to God in every aspect of life cuts right across the Western philosophy in which we are brought up, with its absolute notions of individual freedom to determine what is right and what we should do. Whether it is the decisive get-up-and-go of an entrepreneur, or the pop group The Manic Street Preachers' post-modern 'This is my truth, tell me yours', what counts is the individual's autonomy to decide: 'This is my life—I believe and do what I want and no one can tell me otherwise!' Naturally, Christians do not express it quite so rebelliously and they will pay lip-service to the idea of obedience, at least until it encroaches on an area they wish to keep private and where they won't allow God any say. When this area is approached the barriers go up immediately and the hackles rise. How can God ask that of me? How dare he? And so they cordon off an area of life with security tape—Faith Line: Do Not Cross!— and set up a zone where God is not allowed to go and define a subject that he is not allowed to raise, because only people with security clearance may enter and God is not one of them.

This leads to an almost schizophrenic way of carrying on because it compartmentalizes life into spiritual and non-spiritual portions. I am a Christian on Sunday, but I do not bring my faith to work, so that while I may pray on Sunday, I will also scheme and cheat along with everyone else for the rest of the week. I proclaim dependence upon God on the one hand, and yet on the other live all but one hour a week without any real thought for him (and it is debatable how real that one hour will be). I ask for God's blessing upon everything that I do, but then tell him there are areas of my life that he cannot touch. I am happy for him to patrol the frontiers to make sure the enemy at the gates doesn't get in, but he must also accept that there are certain no-go areas in my territory and he had better respect them. But God will not have it that way and if you look at it from his viewpoint you will soon see why.

In 1967 Albania closed its borders completely. Already allied to the most extreme communist nations of the day, it eventually rejected them when they did not prove extreme enough. Proclaiming itself the world's first atheistic nation it proceeded to shut down all contact with the outside world, so that for the best part of twenty-five years no one knew what was going on. Tourists were permitted to enter in the mid-1980s, but it was only when the borders opened fully in 1991 and foreigners could move in that the disaster became tragically apparent. The country's dictator, Enver Hoxha, in an act of unadulterated paranoia, had wasted what little wealth the nation had in building a vast system of concrete bunkers and tunnels across the countryside. It is estimated that they built about 700,000 of these in a country the size of Wales and that in the process they used enough concrete to house the entire impoverished population of about three million people. The reason given for madness on this scale was that they were needed to protect the nation from outsiders who would come in to steal the country's wealth. Meanwhile, with borders secure and preventing both inbound and outbound traffic, the Albanian people languished in crippling, almost medieval poverty, living in appalling housing and at times suffering conditions—probably starvation, for instance—akin to a Third World disaster zone. Albania is changing rapidly today, but the continued existence of empty, decaying factory buildings, roads with more potholes than tarmac and significant numbers of donkey carts in farming villages all bear witness to a past period of unimaginable deprivation.

That is what your life would look like if God were to respect your wishes and let you keep a portion of it back from him. The borders might be secure, but the rest would be a crumbling ruin, so God deliberately lays claim to the whole lot. There are no no-go areas for him, and if he has to make the point quite dramatically, then he is willing to do so.

Some people get themselves tied into knots over the test that God threw Abraham's way, believing that such a command—to sacrifice Isaac—made him no better than the Canaanite gods whose followers really did sacrifice their children. But that is to miss the point. God is not like the gods of the Canaanites since he stepped in to prevent Abraham killing his son and then throughout Scripture made clear his hatred of such practices. But putting the command in such awful terms was probably the only way of getting the point across: Would Abraham withhold anything from God? Was there anything or anyone in his life over which he would not allow his God to have a controlling interest? Was his son Isaac a no-go area? As we will see, the circumstances surrounding Isaac's birth and his significance for God's plan made it quite likely, for Isaac was not just important; he was indispensable.

An uphill climb

In addition to the spiritual significance of the location of the sacrifice of Isaac—2 Chronicles 3:1 tells us that Moriah was to be the site of the Jewish temple in Jerusalem more than a thousand years later—the nature of the journey appears to mirror the cost of obedience: three days' travel and then an uphill slog to complete it.

Abraham is a model of an obedient response to God's command, in that he got up the next day and left early in the morning for the place God was going to show him. There is, however, no mention of the emotional turmoil he must have been in. It is one thing to *understand* God's will (and although it appears straightforward for Abraham in this case, we must acknowledge that it is not always so for us, since events may point one way and advice another, so we are left with the problem of figuring out what God is saying through the seeming confusion). But it is another thing altogether to *obey* God's will. Mark Twain is reputed to have said 'It's not the parts of the Bible that I don't understand that trouble me, but the parts that I do' and obedience is much like that. The greater struggle is more often with the commands of God that we do understand all too clearly, but would rather not follow. And it is quite another thing to *keep* obeying. I don't know about you, but I have learned that the best way to get something unpleasant done is to do it at the first available opportunity and get it over as quickly as possible. That makes sound practice in every area of life and particularly in obedience to God, since there is nothing worse than going through the day putting off the awful moment by doing other, less important tasks and living with the dread of the one you really need to do. So I summon up my courage and dive in. But if I am prevented from completing what I should do I am in great danger of turning back. Given time to think about it, I am likely to change my mind and not do it.

> We must not pretend that it is easy to keep to the route of obedience.

Spare a thought for Abraham, then. He has obeyed God and set out to sacrifice his son, but the journey has taken three days. That would have been three days in which the thought of turning back would have occurred every half an hour. A monumental battle would have been raging the whole time to preserve his initial determination to do what God wanted. Fortunately, faith and obedience won the day (or rather, the three days) and Abraham did what God required. But we must not pretend that it is easy to keep to the route of obedience. It is easy to be sidetracked, diverted or distracted from the task so that, having won the first battle needed to start to obey, you lose the war of attrition involved in completing the task. The battle to obey God is not won by a single, decisive blow that squashes all resistance at a stroke. The enemy will regroup and attack at a later date.

> The battle to obey God is not won by a single, decisive blow that squashes all resistance at a stroke.

Nor is obedience usually a short sprint to the finish line. A marathon is a much more appropriate illustration, with all its attendant parallels—blisters, cramp, pain, exhaustion and the death of the first man who ran it! The only answer is to pray as much about completing as you do about starting and ask for God's help not to turn back when continued obedience seems futile.

Hand over your valuables!

In a culture that is so totally sold on personal ownership, increasing wealth and amassing possessions, it is very easy to forget that nothing we possess is actually ours. We joke that we can't take it with us when we die, but assume that it is all ours until that point. Christians may go one stage better and accept that God has a right to a tenth of all that they earn, but still believe that the remaining 90% is theirs to do with as they wish. In fact, there is nothing in your life over which you have exclusive rights, whether property, money, possessions, time, even children. This does not mean that God will never allow you any personal property or savings, or forbid you to speak of 'my family' or 'my house', but it does mean that they are not yours alone. I heard a speaker attribute to Edith Schaeffer the saying that you should hold everything you possess lightly, in the open palm of your hand. It is yours for the moment, but the humiliating tussle that is necessary if you hold everything in tightly clenched fists so that God has to prise open your fingers to get it will be avoided.

Of course, unlike Jesus' request to the rich young ruler, God is not asking Abraham for all of his very significant wealth, just his most valued part of it; but even this we struggle with. I guess the reason for this is because we are so much affected by the way our society thinks on this matter. Give God your spare time and your loose change. The leftovers are good enough for him, because they are quite easy to give and cost you nothing, but he will not accept that. From the very earliest time he has pointed out that everything we own comes from him—even the ability to make money and produce wealth—so he has, not surprisingly, required the best from us. For instance, the sacrificial system demanded a young animal in top condition, rather than a mangy, disease-ridden old creature that needed putting out of its misery.

But we are talking about Abraham's most valued possession as if it were a piece of property, an animal or a bank account, when it was in fact his son, Isaac, and there is no real comparison between those two types of valuables. If forced to choose between people

> It is very easy to forget that nothing we possess is actually ours.

or possessions, anyone in their right mind would not hesitate to take the former. When the rectory in Epworth went up in flames in 1709 Samuel and Susannah Wesley led most of the family to safety, but young John Wesley was only plucked from an upstairs window at the last moment before the thatched roof collapsed. Samuel's instant response was to kneel in prayer with the family and give thanks to God, because, even though he had lost everything he possessed, his family had been preserved. So there is no doubt that Abraham would willingly have traded his entire fortune for his son if God had asked him. But he hadn't. He had asked for Isaac.

Let's be clear about this before we go any further. God is not going to ask you to sacrifice your children. As I mentioned earlier, we have specific condemnation in the Bible of the Canaanite practices showing us that child sacrifice is not an option. You cannot lay claim to some fresh piece of revelation from God telling you to do the same as Abraham, when the Bible already tells you that God will not ask this of you. And equally you cannot claim any support from the Bible for abusing or neglecting your children on the grounds that you are conducting an important ministry in the church and that this must come first. But God may pose the same type of question as the one confronting Abraham: Are you withholding your children from him?

It is quite possible to be thoroughly orthodox in what we say at this point, but in practice act quite differently. We may affirm our belief that children are on loan from God and not a permanent endowment; we can state that they are a trust from God and we are stewards of that trust; and we can say that God uses parents to lay the foundation in a child's life and God builds on it the way he chooses. But there is a world of difference between saying that and living by it. It means that we have no rights over our children's future.

If we are honest, our plans for our children die very hard. We naturally have hopes and dreams for them, so that we are happy when they do well and disappointed when they stumble. As they grow up we try to train and encourage them to follow the Lord and serve him, but as they hit adulthood (frequently when they move away to college or for work) we realize that we have no power to enforce what we feel is best and that we must entrust them to God for him to guide them. It is then that we try to bargain with God:

'Lord, I'm happy to give you my child if you tell me what you are going to do with her.'

No deal. I don't tell you what I am going to do with you, so why should I tell you your child's future?

'I understand that, but you must understand that I only want the best for my child.'

*And you must understand that **I know** what is best for your child and can actually give it to her.*

'I accept that, but I don't want her to throw her life away.'

Don't you trust me?

'Yes, but you might take her to the other end of the country.'

Or to the other side of the world, perhaps?

'Over my dead body!'

Be careful what you are saying.

It is humbling to realize that Christian parents can sometimes prove to be the biggest obstacles to their children's spiritual growth and service because they will not let go of them, and there is nothing quite like the prospect of the child becoming a missionary to reveal the hidden strings. Just let a young woman, training to be a lawyer, announce that she is giving all that up to go to be a Bible translator; or a young man state that he is abandoning a successful career in business to join a church planting team and the real state of affairs may suddenly appear. Whether it is the thought of not seeing them or the grandchildren for years on end that causes the opposition, or perhaps the concern that they will throw away good prospects (read: marriage, family, a career with lots of money), or whether these are just excuses, the effect is that parents find themselves unable to accept what God is doing with their children.

> It is humbling to realize that Christian parents can sometimes prove to be the biggest obstacles to their children's spiritual growth and service because they will not let go of them, and there is nothing quite like the prospect of the child becoming a missionary to reveal the hidden strings.

Isobel Kuhn, in the first of her autobiographical books *By Searching*, recounts the opposition she faced from her mother to her intention of going to China as a missionary. Although her mother was a believer, she remained implacable, refused to give her blessing to her daughter's training and informed her that it would be over her dead body that she left. It was. She died shortly before Isobel departed and, although the book tells us that she was reconciled during her last illness both to her daughter and her daughter's plans, it nevertheless contains an element of bitter tragedy that it took terminal illness to make her release her grip on her daughter and accept what was happening.

I realize that not all children go the right way and that it is sometimes obvious that they are on a dangerous path, so parents may feel they have the right to resist their children's proposals, but the principle must remain the same in all cases. It is bad psychology to try to force your children to go your way into adulthood, since it cramps, frustrates and embitters them, as well as probably twisting you into knots. But psychology is not the point here. Rather, it is that it is bad from a spiritual point of view to try to force *God* to take your children the way you want them to go. You and I are not in a position to make demands of God that he do one thing and not the other with them. We can do nothing but place them into his care and trust him with them, whatever that means for their future, success or failure, great deeds or none. That will not be easy. A number of years ago a Christian friend said to me that surrendering her hopes for her son, who is autistic and will never be what she imagined for him, was one of the hardest things she had ever done. When he was born, she and her husband had prayed over him and committed him to the Lord, asking that he would be a man of God, but his condition meant that their dreams would not be realized. She came across a line in a hymn that she had previously sung without thinking about, but which suddenly leapt out with a force that stunned her: 'Perish every fond ambition, all I've ever sought and hoped and known.'[2] Years later, she can see that, although he has not done the things she had expected a spiritual young man to do, he is not the failure she feared he would become and has a valid ministry of his own, but it was very hard at the time to relinquish her plans and aspirations for him. She probably had no choice in the matter, but it was a good thing that she did let go.

So what do you value more—your relationship with God or the gifts he has given you? Do you worship God just because he is God, or perhaps

So what do you value more—your relationship with God or the gifts he has given you?

because he has given you a child? Is it possible that your child, whom you love, comes between you and God? Give me your son, Abraham.

Dispensing with the indispensable

We must press the matter still further, since it was not just a question of Abraham letting God have the son he loved. The truth is that Abraham could not manage without Isaac. Words like 'vital' and 'essential' spring to mind, even 'indispensable', because without Isaac, Abraham's family had no future. The writer to the Hebrews captures the dilemma: 'He who had received the promises was about to sacrifice his one and only son, even though God had said to him, "It is through Isaac that your offspring will be reckoned"' (Hebrews 11:17–18).

God had made promises to Abraham that he would give him the land of Canaan, make him into a great nation and through him bless the whole world. This obviously required children which Abraham did not have initially, but God made it clear that he would give him a son by his wife Sarah and that this child would be the one through whom the promises would be fulfilled. This promised child was Isaac, and God confirmed in Genesis 21:12 that everything rested on him: 'It is through Isaac …' Yet now in Genesis 22, God is telling Abraham to sacrifice him! The dilemma should be evident. If Isaac were lost, then the promises would fail. Abraham's family would have no future with God. There would be no nation to take the land. No blessing to the world. And we know from our perspective that there would be no Saviour. And no salvation. Isaac really was indispensable.

If anyone had the right to turn round to God and tell him to back off, Abraham was the one. He could quite easily have told God that Isaac was untouchable, but it is here that Abraham's faith shines through. He obeys in the belief that God will take care of the consequences of his obedience. When they reach the base of the mountain he leaves his servants with the instruction that he and Isaac would go up to worship and then '*we* will come back to you'—not just one of them. The writer of the letter to the Hebrews says that Abraham's thinking behind this remark was that he 'reasoned that God could raise the dead', and then adds that, figuratively speaking, Isaac was raised from the dead (Hebrews 11:19). In addition, when they were climbing the mountain, Isaac asked where the lamb for the sacrifice was, to which Abraham replied that God would provide it, which he did in the end with a ram caught by its horns in a thicket. At each point, Abraham answered the doubts with faith, and his faith was vindicated.

The parallels with the suffering and death of the Lord Jesus Christ at this point are too striking to avoid mentioning. God the Father could quite easily have told us that his Son was off-limits and that salvation would have to come by another route, even though no such alternative existed. He could have reminded us that he had never been parted from his Son through all eternity, during which they had enjoyed an unbroken and perfect relationship of love, so for the Son to leave and come to earth to save us would be too much to ask. But he sent him and, moreover, did not spare him. Just as Isaac carried the wood (willingly—that must say something about his faith, too) and Abraham carried the fire and the knife, so Jesus willingly carried the cross, while the Father put him to death for our sins. The lamb was provided for Abraham to sacrifice in the place of his son, Isaac, and a saying came out of this event to the effect that 'on the mountain of the Lord it will be provided' (Genesis 22:14). On another hill, Calvary, God provided the sacrifice for our sins in the person of his Son, Jesus Christ. There was no lamb for him that day to die in his place, for he was the Lamb of God whose duty it was to die in the place of sinners all over the world. Isaac could be spared, but Jesus could not.

> When God asks you to surrender something to him, he is therefore not asking anything of you that he has not already given himself.

When God asks you to surrender something to him, he is therefore not asking anything of you that he has not already given himself. He gave everything in giving Jesus so that you and I might be reconciled to him, in a loving relationship with him. If he asks you to give something up it is in order to preserve that relationship with him and ensure that it grows deeper—and a little thought will tell you that God is the one who is really indispensable, not the things he gives us. When Abraham went to the point of sacrificing his son he demonstrated that there was nothing between him and God, and that he would not allow anything to get in the way of this relationship.

If, however, you live for something other than God it is quite likely that you will end up regarding that thing as indispensable and be unable to part with it. It is not for me to say what that thing might be in your case, but I know what some people's are. Some regard the church building as inviolable. Their very lives are woven into its fabric, having been brought up in its shadow, so that its forms and traditions, the very bricks even, cannot be touched. To alter anything so fundamental is like demolishing a piece not merely of history, but of their own person. Suggestions that a room be remodelled is like recommending amputation. The reason for this is that they have invested personal capital in the church building and anything so radical as sale or demolition comes like a personal attack, so they hold the future to ransom because they cannot let go of the past. Others rest in the way the church has done things in the past and cannot see the good in new ways of doing things. Still others live for what they can do in the church's ministry. Take that from them and they lose their reason for living. We have all heard of the aged choirmaster who has been in his post for fifty years and needs to retire (and the congregation needs him to retire, too!), but no one has the heart to break the news to him because they know how he will feel. But old people are not the only ones who can get stuck in this rut of needing something else other than God. Young people can be caught up with having fun—take the fun out of life and faith withers. Then again I knew a farmer who committed suicide because a stroke prevented him from continuing the farming that had been his whole life—ironically it became his death, too. Nor are ministers exempt from living for their ministry rather than living for God. It was instructive to read a comment from Martyn Lloyd-Jones, made during what was his last illness and when he was unable to do the one thing he was most famous for: 'People say to me it must be very trying for you not to be able to preach—No! Not at all. I was not living upon preaching.'[3] It can be anything—family, money, success, fame, traditions, excitement, work … The effect is the same: they will all keep you from a close relationship with God and they may actually damage it irreparably. Nothing should be indispensable except knowing God himself.

> Nothing should be indispensable except knowing God himself.

When I wrote to my girlfriend and finished our relationship I did so without any thought of ever seeing her again; but a couple of months later she started attending church and was converted shortly afterwards. Later that year we started going out again, but this time on a different footing, and a few years after that we were married. The challenge of God's test of Abraham is that you must be prepared to let go. Entrust it to him, whatever it is, being ready for him to take it from you if he so wishes, believing that he knows whether it really is indispensable and that he will help you live without it, if it comes to that. And it is possible that, as with Isaac, you may receive it back again.

Summary: Obedience is the heart of faith.

Key verse: Genesis 22:12: 'Now I know that you fear God, because you have not withheld from me your son, your only son.'

To think about: Is there anything in my life that is assuming such importance that it is overshadowing my relationship with God? How am I going to deal with that?

'Does the LORD delight in burnt offerings and sacrifices as much as in obeying the voice of the LORD? To obey is better than sacrifice', 1 Samuel 15:22.

'This is love for God: to obey his commands. And his commands are not burdensome', 1 John 5:3.

Thinking more deeply

My child, I am asking you to love me first, more than anything or anyone. I ask you to love me with all your heart and soul and strength and mind. For this is exactly the kind of love with which I love you. I have gone to the place appointed. I have gone up the mountain with my Son. He carried the cross, but I carried the knife and I bound him there and smote him there, the Lamb of God that takes away the sin of the world. I love you like that. I am not asking from you anything I have not given myself. My son, my daughter, give me your heart. If I love you like that, can you not surrender those worthless toys that you cling on to so much? If I love you like that, can you not persevere in that work for me, continue to nurse that person for me, or give over that friendship? I gave you my Son, may I not ask for the best years of your life on earth? Can I not take your son for my service across the world? Am I really asking too much?

Denis Lane, *A Man and his God.*

Notes

1 **Denis Lane,** *A Man and his God* (Welwyn: Evangelical Press, 1981), p. 149.
2 **Henry Francis Lyte,** 'Jesus, I my cross have taken'.
3 **Iain Murray,** *David Martyn Lloyd-Jones: The Fight of Faith 1939–1981* (Edinburgh: The Banner of Truth Trust, 1990), p. 739.

4 Alone:
Left to your own devices

Managing when the props are removed

To walk in darkness … is not an indication that they have missed the will of God but is, as for the Servant, intrinsic to the life of obedience (Alec Motyer, Commentary on Isaiah 50).

Please read 2 Chronicles 32:24–33.

I had a friend who once described the evangelism training he received in the Salvation Army. It was of the 'sink or swim' variety. A bus would take a large group of trainees out, depositing them one by one at regular intervals on street corners, returning after half an hour or so to pick them up. During its absence trainees were on their own and had to lead their own evangelistic services in whatever way they felt appropriate. Sing, read the Scriptures, pray, preach, engage people in conversation—they could do whatever they wanted. I did something similar when I was a student and I have to say that it was the longest half-hour of my life. Even sitting in the dentist's chair goes quicker! What was so unnerving was that being on my own left me very vulnerable and liable to cave in under pressure. All my courage evaporated, my mind went blank when talking to people and I began to wish I could change into something small and crawl away. I discovered that there is nothing quite like being left on your own to see how you will manage.

Of course, I know that there is a sense in which we are never alone, for Jesus tells us that he will never forsake us and that we have his Holy Spirit to be with us for ever. But there are times when we do not feel that he is with us and as a result have the sense that we are alone—doing street evangelism was just such an occasion for me. In a way, that is what happened to Hezekiah. The writer of 2 Chronicles tells us in 32:31 that 'God left him to test him and to know everything that was in his heart', and he buckled under pressure.

But I am running ahead of myself. Let's begin at the beginning.

A devastating prognosis

When a serious illness struck Hezekiah at the age of thirty-nine he sent for the prophet Isaiah. We know nothing of Isaiah's medical skills, but Hezekiah evidently reckoned that he would know what God would have to say in response to his prayers for healing. He did. He bluntly informed Hezekiah that he was not going to recover, but would soon die.

Hezekiah was devastated. You can read his wailing prayer in Isaiah 38, along with a description of his shattered feelings at receiving such bad news. I don't think it is inaccurate to summarize his response as: 'It's not fair! I've worked so hard for you that I shouldn't be dying so young!'

That is hardly the response of faith to a crisis, even if it is perfectly understandable. Panicking like that is what we would expect of unbelievers (who often reason that if you're not panicking it only shows you don't understand the gravity of the situation), but not of a good man who trusts God and has already experienced God's real help in amazing ways. It serves to show that we need to pray for God's help to be given in sudden crises before they arrive, asking that God would sustain us in the hour of need and help us to respond in quiet trust and submission to God.

For all its selfishness, Hezekiah's desperate prayer was, nevertheless, answered. I guess this was rather a surprise to Isaiah, since he was leaving the palace at the time—he was probably going to write a funeral sermon— and had to be called back by the Lord to give this news to the king. The previous message was dramatically reversed, the illness was healed and the king was granted fifteen more years of life. Moreover, at Hezekiah's request a miraculous sign—something happening to the sun—was given to prove that this would take place.

While it is not good to witness such a loss of faith in a man of God, it is comforting to see that God still answered him. It is reassuring that God hears even the most incoherent of prayers, those made perhaps with a sense of despair, spoken through crushing grief, and that he is not deaf to our cries of anguish; but we are justified in asking whether Hezekiah learned anything from it. I know a minister who served as a hospital chaplain in a mining town and met countless numbers of seriously injured miners who prayed in their fear when threatened with major surgery. Many solemnly resolved to change their ways, start coming to church and live for God, if only he would ensure they recovered. Yet once they were healthy and out of hospital all turned their back on God, and not one ever turned up at church.

Hezekiah's initial response to the illness and answered prayer for healing appears to have been favourable. Isaiah's account of these events has a psalm that the king wrote after his healing and it is full of praise to God. We might think that here is a man with a new spiritual resolve; the panic has subsided and the king is back to normal. Yet our narrator in Chronicles gives a rather pessimistic summary: 'But Hezekiah's heart was proud and he did not respond to the kindness shown him' (32:25). The events that follow reveal what he is talking about.

Seduced by flattery

Hard on the heels of Hezekiah's illness and recovery came a deputation of Babylonian envoys. At the time, 702 B.C., Babylon was in revolt against the Assyrians who ruled the Near East. The Babylonians had given their oppressors a run for their money but were now on the brink of defeat, so came to Jerusalem with the pretext of finding out 'about the miraculous sign that had occurred in the land' (32:3–13), but more likely it was with a view to secure last-ditch support from Hezekiah for the rebellion.

Hezekiah had good reason to join the rebellion. In his religious reformation of the nation (which you can read about in 2 Chronicles 29–31) he had trashed the Assyrian gods his father Ahaz had previously installed when he formed a disastrous alliance with Assyria, so it is safe to say Hezekiah was not popular in Nineveh, Assyria's capital city. The Assyrians had not yet called him to account for his actions, since they had troubles elsewhere, but he knew it would not be long before they turned up. Why not, therefore, join the rebellion and get rid of the Assyrians once and for all? From a military perspective it made sense.

But it was not as simple as that. The Scriptures are filled with statements about the power of God to fight for his people, along with exhortations to trust him rather than their own strength or military might. Israel's history, however, while it gives numerous examples of such deliverance, also contains many instances of their failure to trust God and the sad consequences of such failures. This is one such instance.

Here is the crunch. Would Hezekiah give glory to God and trust him alone to keep them safe when the empire struck back, or would he put his trust in someone else's armies? You don't have to look far to see that he had every reason to place his faith in God: God had kept the Assyrians occupied elsewhere during his reformation of the nation; he had brought rapid and widespread success to this movement of religious reform; he had given Hezekiah incredible riches; and now God had answered prayer, not only saving Hezekiah from death, but also displaying his control over the heavens in such a way that the sky-watching Babylonian astronomers sat up and took note. How could Hezekiah *not* trust God?

> Would Hezekiah give glory to God and trust him alone to keep them safe when the empire struck back, or would he put his trust in someone else's armies?

But he didn't. When Hezekiah should have politely shown the Babylonian diplomats the door, Isaiah tells us he showed them everything in his palace. That was tantamount to placing everything at their disposal and throwing his lot in with the rebellion. Rather than trust God to keep the scourge of the Near East at bay, he joined up with a crowd who would, in the long run, prove more damaging to Israel than anyone else. It was a bad move spiritually, and it turned out that it was not much smarter from a military perspective either. The rebellion was defeated that same year and the Assyrians laid siege to Jerusalem in the next. What had he been thinking?

The three accounts that we have of this incident give us some clear indications of what was going on. The writer of Chronicles puts it quite bluntly: *his heart became proud*. He had received so much from God— there is an impressive list in the Chronicles account—that it went to his head. Perhaps he was flattered by the thought that the Babylonians appeared to need his help. That would give him importance that no king of Israel or Judah had enjoyed since the days of David and Solomon. It would give him a great name in the annals of the nation's history. Can you imagine the titles and accolades he would receive? Hezekiah the Godly, Restorer of the Faith; Hezekiah the Valiant, Judah's Warrior King and Conqueror of God's Enemies. I can see him strutting around his palace with his Babylonian guests meekly in tow, his chest puffed out with pride at the thought of the glory that was coming his way. It is a variant on the selfish despair he felt at the thought of losing it all when he was ill and dying. And as if to confirm this, Isaiah tells us of his reaction to another message from God once the Babylonians had left (Isaiah 39).

The second message informed him that the treasures he had been showing off to the diplomats from Babylon would end up in Babylon one day, when the nation was defeated, its wealth plundered and carried off into exile. Hezekiah, however, does not seem unduly perturbed by this revelation and displays quite a shocking lack of concern (Isaiah 39:8). 'At least it won't happen in my lifetime', was the essence of what he thought about the message. Is this the same man who had changed the nation just fifteen years earlier? His reforming zeal seems to have left him. True concern for the nation's spiritual welfare that he had displayed at the beginning of his reign would have led him to take further action to strengthen the nation's hold on God. Josiah after him, for instance, on learning of God's anger upon the nation, instituted far-reaching reforms in the belief that God would show mercy to those who repented, and not bring disaster. But Hezekiah appeared to resign himself to the inevitable with a show of pious submission that was in reality a mask for callous and selfish indifference. Perhaps it is not surprising that his son Manasseh, one of the worst kings in all of Judah's history, was born and grew up during this extra fifteen years granted to Hezekiah.

At our best we are inconsistent and unreliable, with blind spots and weak points, and no more so when our egos are being massaged. There is something universally appealing about someone—friend or enemy—who pays us a compliment. But there is also nothing quite so dangerous as being surrounded by yes-men and toadies. The trouble with being a celebrity (or, in Hezekiah's case, a king) is that sooner or later you begin to believe all the good things that are said about you, whether they are true or not. This smokescreen of flattery inevitably clouds judgement and in this instance led Hezekiah to form a disastrous alliance with people he should have avoided. The English proverb states that 'pride comes before a fall', but it is not a true quotation of the Bible. 'Pride goes before destruction' is the Bible's version, and it is frighteningly accurate. None of us is immune to temptation in this area, so vigilance can be our only response. Watch yourself!

Standing on your own

There is an extra detail that the writer of 2 Chronicles adds that is of key importance and seems to explain the reason for everything that happened. He tells us that when the Babylonians turned up, God 'left [Hezekiah] to test him and to know everything that was in his heart.' In other words, Hezekiah found himself alone that day with the Babylonian ambassadors in a way he had not known before, and their tantalizing offer proved too much for him to resist.

We need to be clear what this does not mean. It is not saying that God abandoned Hezekiah, rejected him, or callously manipulated him into a corner to force him to make a mistake. What it does mean is harder to say, but one feature of the account appears significant. Isaiah was not present at the meeting and only appeared once the ambassadors had gone home. It is very likely that Hezekiah had previously leaned heavily upon Isaiah both for counsel and support for the reformation, so perhaps God sent Isaiah away that day to oblige Hezekiah to answer the temptation in his own words and thus provide answers about his true spiritual state. Was Isaiah's wisdom resident in Hezekiah's life? Had the king really learned to trust God as a result of the breathtaking answers to prayer he had experienced? We might ask, was he standing on his own two feet? It is the sort of thing that young Christians experience when they go to university. Cut loose from parental restraints and guidance, they have to learn to express faith for themselves rather than rely on others, and it is not an easy time for many. Sadly, Hezekiah's experience of flying solo in this way was equally turbulent and, in the absence of a trusted counsellor, he made a very poor landing.

If you read the first two chapters of the book of Job you see something similar taking place. Satan could not believe that Job's faith was genuine since God had given him so much. He cynically reckoned that Job would turn against God if his prosperity was stripped from him, so God gave Satan permission to test this theory out. Job lost everything, from his family to his health, and the support of his wife and friends. What made matters worse was that God was inexplicably absent and much of this difficult book details the debates between Job and his friends. The friends reasoned that God must be punishing him for some unconfessed sin, but he maintained that he was innocent; yet he could not explain why God was distant. It was a titanic struggle for Job, but he held fast to his faith in God and was proved right in the end. God had not deserted him, but had been silent for a little while.

In these two examples there is a similar process at work. It is as if God has taken a step back from believers' lives and permitted difficult circumstances to enter, in order to reveal what lies beneath the surface of their lives—what is in their hearts, as the writer of 2 Chronicles puts it. In Job's case, the question Satan posed about Job's relationship to God is one that can always be asked where money, power and gifts are involved: how do rich people know that their friends are genuine and not just in it for what they can get out of it? The only way to find out is to remove the benefits of the friendship for a short time and see what happens. And in Hezekiah's case, the only way of knowing whether he had learned enough from the blessings of the past to trust God rather than the Babylonians was to make him answer for himself for once.

> This is sometimes the way God deals with his people, when he removes the props they had previously depended on and forces them to stand alone.

Disconcerting as it might seem, this is sometimes the way God deals with his people, when he removes the props they had previously depended on and forces them to stand alone. It may be that he takes away colleagues at work who have been a great support, so that you find yourself the only Christian in the office. Friends who have been such an inspiration in church life move away. Or God may seem to distance himself from you. Have you ever experienced times in which you feel spiritually dry? Prayer shrivels up because God feels far away, neither seeming to answer nor even listen. The Bible suddenly becomes uninteresting and reading it becomes a drudge.

Church activities drag and take on the feeling of a duty to be endured. And you become weary and worn down, losing enthusiasm for what once excited you. New Christians find it hard to believe that this can possibly happen, so experiencing such desolation can be a prelude to terrible doubt: I shouldn't be feeling like this. Was I just fooling myself? Am I even a Christian?

It has to be acknowledged that there may be other reasons why you might be feeling like this, so it is always right to examine yourself to see if there is any cause in you. If you have sinned you will have to deal with this first, because only repentance will bring forgiveness, restoration and an awareness of reconciliation. Another equally important factor within you may be your own health. Stress, depression, illness, fatigue or conflict at home, to name but a few factors, will all affect the way you feel about your relationship with God. Take the eighteenth century hymn writer William Cowper as an example. Many of his hymns express a desperate longing for God to return and you can use them to put your own repentance into words. However, you see them in a different light when you realize that they were written by a man who was profoundly depressed much of the time and did not sense the presence of God as a result. There is no doubting the genuineness of his faith, but his depression ensured he did not *feel* the reality of it. He felt God was absent and spent much of his time lamenting it, so we must recognize that we may be similarly influenced by an upset in body chemistry.

But this may not be the case at all. You may look at yourself and believe that you have no reason in yourself to be struggling the way you are, so it is quite possible that you are experiencing what is outlined in Hezekiah's case. God is testing you to see what is in your heart by removing all the props and letting you stand alone in the dark for a while.

What is in your heart?

In one of Aesop's fables a fox tries in vain to reach a bunch of grapes hanging on a wall, and when it gives up in disgust its parting comment is that the grapes were sour anyway. People naturally do the same with God. If he doesn't answer immediately they accuse him of not caring and turn away to look for other alternatives. Much of Jesus' teaching in the parables is designed to sift out those who are merely curious about him from those who will search wholeheartedly for the truth, and a time of testing will have the same effect. God will use it to know what is in your heart and whether you are going to be like so many who will follow only so long as the going is easy. Will you trust him in the darkness, or give up on him? Will you accuse him of abandoning you, or will you hold on until he returns to you?

Alternatively, if you find yourself alone will you take a stand for God, or buckle under the pressure from friends and colleagues to tone down your beliefs and compromise your faith? John Stott describes some believers as 'rabbit-hole Christians', who dash from the safety of one cosy warren to another—prayer meetings, coffee with housegroup members, support groups, church committees—and congratulate themselves that they have got through another day unscathed, but who never really make contact with the unbelieving world. What happens if you are the only rabbit in a room full of foxes?

I would suggest—blind panic aside—that there are a number of things you should learn from this sort of situation, and that you should aim to grow from it.

REALIZE HOW MUCH YOU NEED HIM

It is possible to make a statement that is true, but say it too easily; statements about needing God can fall into this category. In reality we know very little about what it means to depend absolutely on God. For instance, the Lord's Prayer with its request for daily bread means little to us in a society where we stockpile food to such an extent that we have to throw millions of tons of it away every year. But for the Judean peasant, as also for billions of the world's poor today, daily bread required daily faith. Paid only at the end of the day, he received just one day's wages, enough to put food on the table the next day, but that was all. A day without work meant the next day without food. That required faith in itself, but the real dependence on God came on the Sabbath. With no work at all permitted on the Sabbath—and therefore no spare cash—the poor were in God's hands for what they would eat the next day. I have never been that close to the breadline, but that does not completely invalidate what I can learn from finding myself alone and apparently without God. Such an experience forces me to confront reality and ask whether I really meant what I said, and I discover just how helpless I am and that I really do need him.

My first Sunday preaching engagement from Bible college went very well. I was still quite a young Christian at the time and had been particularly nervous about it, so I was therefore pleasantly surprised when I felt God's help in preaching and it was well received. On the way home on the London Underground a verse from John 15 came to my mind: 'Apart from me you can do nothing' (v. 5). When I got back to college I thought about the significance of this verse and felt it was a message from the Lord: 'Don't think you did that on your own. You need me more than you can imagine.' I prayed over it and acknowledged my dependence upon the Lord, believing that I had learned and understood what the Lord was saying. Three weeks later, however, I learned it at a deeper level altogether.

I was to preach a series of four messages over four Sundays in another church, but the first went so badly that I nearly cancelled the other three. It simply fell apart before my eyes. What had appeared coherent in preparation suddenly didn't make sense and I found it impossible to explain what I had in my notes. Tongue-tied—and seemingly brain-dead, too—I struggled on for twenty minutes, desperately wanting to finish quickly, but, short of dissolving into a tearful heap on the platform, I couldn't work out how to do so. I was on my own—and the pulpit is a very lonely place when that happens. On the way home that afternoon the same verse came home to me: 'Apart from me you can do nothing.' Relearning that in the darkness was a very effective way of bringing home the truth that I had only partially grasped beforehand.

REMEMBER THAT GOD REMAINS FAITHFUL

It may come as a surprise to realize that the siege of Jerusalem by the Assyrians took place *after* the visit of the Babylonians, because all the accounts place it before (e.g. 2 Chronicles 32:1–23). This is probably because they took their cue from Isaiah who arranged his material in thematic, rather than chronological, order. Thus, Isaiah chapters 36 and 37 bring to an end the long section on prophecies about Assyria by detailing the defeat of the siege. And chapters 39 and 40 start a new section that has the Babylonian exile as its focus, so he begins with his first prophecy of that exile. What we fail to notice in this reordering of the account is that there is good news even in Hezekiah's failure.

We know that the Assyrians defeated the Babylonians shortly after the diplomats' fateful visit to Jerusalem and that they then swept down upon Judah the next year, quickly capturing all of the fortified cities except Jerusalem. The three descriptions we have of the siege of Jerusalem give an idea of the suffering of the people and just how close Hezekiah came to total defeat—he initially paid tribute to the Assyrian king. Yet in a complete reversal of expectations God stepped in and answered the Assyrian general's arrogant and insulting challenge that compared the Lord to the defeated gods of other downtrodden peoples. A diversion caused by an Egyptian army was followed by plague in the Assyrian camp, which ensured that both the siege and the threat to Hezekiah's reforms were lifted. Subsequently the Assyrian king returned to his homeland where he was murdered by two of his sons in an attempted coup.

> Hezekiah failed to trust God, but God did not fail Hezekiah.

Put plainly, Hezekiah failed to trust God, but God did not fail Hezekiah. Then, in his hour of greatest need, Hezekiah prayed that God would help them because they were at the point of collapse, and God miraculously intervened.

HOLD ON IN FAITH AND WAIT FOR HIM

My nightmare in the pulpit only lasted twenty nerve-jangling, sweat-dripping minutes, and it did more than just make me change my shirt as soon as I returned to college. In a way I have never forgotten, it demonstrated my real need of the Holy Spirit's help in ministering the Word of God. Even though I believe I am a better speaker now than I was then, if I am to speak (or write) in a way that will cause men and women to grow spiritually, I still must have the Spirit's power upon my words. I may have the experience to be able to avoid the floundering repetition of someone who does not know what to say, but I will be no more effective. I need his help just as much now.

But twenty minutes is hardly a long time in God's book and it is quite likely that you may find yourself flying solo a whole lot longer. There is nothing immediate you can do about this, except take to heart words that Isaiah 50:10 has for everyone in this situation:

Who among you fears the Lord
    and obeys the word of his servant?
Let him who walks in the dark,
    who has no light,
trust in the name of the Lord,
    and rely on his God.

Isaiah offers no easy way out, other than to trust God in the darkness and continue to believe that he is one who can be relied on. It is interesting to note that the next verse contains quite a severe warning about the temptation to create your own light in this darkness and take what looks like an easy way out and go your own way without him. It is better to be waiting in the darkness—with all its struggles, unhappiness, doubts, temptations—than to be off on a route down which God has not sent you. You must trust him and wait. The bus will return to pick you up again.

> It is better to be waiting in the darkness—with all its struggles, unhappiness, doubts, temptations—than to be off on a route down which God has not sent you.

Summary: God sometimes leaves us to work on our own for a time.

Key verse: Isaiah 50:10: 'Who among you fears the Lord and obeys the word of his servant? Let him who walks in the dark, who has no light, trust in the name of the Lord, and rely on his God.'

To think about: What sort of experience will best help you see how much you need the Lord and thus increase your faith in him?

'The crucible for silver and the furnace for gold, but the Lord tests the heart', Proverbs 17:3.

'At my first defence, no one came to my support, but everyone deserted me … But the Lord stood at my side and gave me strength', 2 Timothy 4:16.

Thinking more deeply

On Hezekiah's response to Isaiah's announcement of God's judgement after the visit of the Babylonian envoys:

What a wretched response from Hezekiah! The earlier oracle (38:1) is as categorical as the prediction here in 39:5–7, yet it was found to be pliant under the pressure of prayer and tears (38:5). But the king has been given a chance to play politics in the first league and he was not now going to return to the 'milk and water' of true religion. When pride replaces humility, self-satisfaction replaces concern for others, and works replace faith, then the die is cast and the kingdom is doomed. When the word of God is met with smugness instead of tears and prayers, the word proves its obduracy and accomplishes its grim purposes.

Alec Motyer, *Commentary on Isaiah (39).*

It is a most sad thing for a gracious heart to lose the face and presence of God and Christ, to be deserted and forsaken by Christ. Yea, I do not know of any thing, or affliction, that is so afflictive to a gracious heart as this: for, take any other affliction, and though it be great, yet it is but a particular affliction, the loss of some particular good, and the putting out of some one candle, or the hiding of some one star; but if Christ hide his face, and God withdraw or hide himself, it is the darkening of the sun, which brings universal darkness upon the soul. It embitters all other afflictions, for as the presence of Christ sweetens all other comforts, so the absence, or forsakings, of Christ embitters all other sufferings, and cuts off all our relief and remedy against them.

William Bridge, *A lifting up for the downcast.*

Part 2
Feeling the heat—real people under pressure

5 Setbacks:
A turn for the worse?

When it all goes belly up

Faith's most severe tests come not when we see nothing, but when we see a stunning array of evidence that seems to prove our faith vain (Elisabeth Elliott, These Strange Ashes).

Please read Philippians 1:12–30.

'It's a fat lot of good believing in God if he leaves you high and dry like that.' I was labouring to explain to my slightly cynical, but basically confused, friend about my reasons for leaving a particular job and this had been his bemused reaction. I had tried to say that I was not at the mercy of events, nor had I suffered an irreversible setback, but rather it was God who was leading me this way, even though I didn't know why, nor where he was heading. My friend sighed, nodded in a 'if that's what you feel but I don't understand you' sort of way, and remarked that he wouldn't really want God for a friend if this was the way he treated us.

I was not the first Christian (nor will I be the last) to be unable to clarify why I felt I had arrived at a roadblock, placed there by God, across my path in life. Any period in which life appears to take a turn for the worse is difficult for Christians in quite a different way than for those who do not believe. While the unbelieving world simply takes it all as more evidence of God's powerlessness or non-existence, you and I have to wrestle with the thorny questions of where God is, what he is or isn't doing and why, and answer those questions in the context of faith in God, not rejection of him. You'll find many psalms that express this dilemma—Why? When? How?—and the very fact that we find these questions in the Old Testament hymn book indicates that God takes them seriously, but that does not mean they are easy to explain.

If anyone had the right to feel that events had taken a spectacular turn for the worse, it was Paul. Here he is writing in chains to the Philippian church after a string of what we would call unmitigated disasters that would lead the most upbeat observer to conclude that God had turned his back on Paul. Consider this brief itinerary and see if you can discern where you think God helped him (or otherwise).

It all began when Paul made a visit to Jerusalem to visit the church there and was nearly lynched by a mob who thought he had brought Gentiles with him into the temple, thereby defiling their most holy site. Saved from certain death by the Roman soldiers who garrisoned the city (no trouble seeing the hand of God there!), he was then held for questioning before being bundled off to the governor (that must be God, too, affording him protection from the Jewish authorities). But this man held Paul for two years, waiting for a bribe that Paul never gave (two years? What's going on?). When the new governor was appointed at the end of this period (this must be God's timing for Paul's release), instead of freeing Paul, he left him in jail in order to ingratiate himself with the Jews (Lord, I thought you were able to direct the thoughts of leaders?). Paul was eventually constrained to appeal to Caesar, fearing he would be handed over to the Jews (couldn't you deliver him, Lord?), so was packed off to Rome to plead his case before the emperor (what about the plan for world mission?). En route he was shipwrecked (but at least he survived that) and once in Rome was held under house arrest for two more years. (What's that in total? Four and a half or five years? Talk about setbacks.) And it is not as if his troubles have ended. As he writes he is still being detained and is under threat of death (Paul, has anything gone right these past years?). To all intents and purposes, it looks like Paul's mission has failed.

It is significant that while Paul acknowledges the apparent setbacks he has suffered, he does not allow them to mask his faith in God's absolute control over his life. We would file reports about these events under a section marked 'Do not open: Faith-destroying material', but he takes a different view of it all. There is no doubt that his faith was tested by what had happened (he was human, after all), but in these verses Paul displays an outlook that lifted him above the doubts we often feel.

God has your life in his hands

EVENTS ARE NOT CHANCE-DRIVEN

Everything around may appear to be outright disaster, but Paul sees matters quite differently. All of his words breathe out a basic confidence in God, that God is master of the situation and that blind fate has not been in operation. Rather like the book of Esther, in which God is not mentioned but the overriding theme is of God's timely deliverance of the Jews from destruction, so Paul does not immediately mention any idea of God's control. But his convictions shine through later[1]—that he is not at the mercy of events, but is in God's hands.

And so are you.

> All of his words breathe out a basic confidence in God, that God is master of the situation and that blind fate has not been in operation.

It is vital that you are convinced about this, because if you listen too much to people who do not approach life from a believing standpoint, sooner or later you will share their sense of helplessness. In his book *The Purpose Driven Life* Rick Warren asks you to define your 'life metaphor'—what is the view of life that you hold in your mind that describes how you think life works? Is it a party, a battle, a race, a roller coaster ride, or perhaps a puzzle? If you listen to some people they will tell you that life is totally out of control: you are in free fall, unable to alter your direction of travel (downwards, too fast) and it is just a matter of time before you hit the ground, so you might as well enjoy it while you can. Others picture life as a lottery: one day your number comes up and there is nothing you can do about it. Still others draw their life metaphor from evolutionary thinking: life is a random series of accidents—*you* are a cosmic accident—without reason or direction. The life metaphor is a useful concept, but make sure that yours includes God and doesn't shut him out. You (and everything else) are in God's hands.

EVENTS WILL NOT JUST 'TURN OUT ALL RIGHT IN THE END'!

In popular philosophy events 'turn out all right in the end' and that is the nearest most people get to the idea of God's rule over the world that we call providence. But in reality it is miles away, since it is expressed as a sincere hope without any assurance of anything good happening at all. It is a fervent desire, spoken to reassure the sufferer of support or sympathy, but nothing more. Yet Paul's words are more than just a pious wish. He is confident that something good will come—has indeed already come—out of apparent disaster, not because events work themselves out, but because *God* works them out. That is his conviction at the end of Romans 8, particularly in verse 28 in which he states that God is able to bring good out of all events for those who love him, and it is no different here for Paul in prison.

YOU ARE WHERE GOD WANTS YOU

This means that you are not where you are by accident. Paul's conviction is firm: 'Knowing that I am put here …' (1:16). The route had been a hard one, and his lodgings were far from comfortable, but that does not shake him in his knowledge that God had brought him to this place. Read the dramatic account in Acts 27–28 that describes how Paul actually got to Rome, and then interpret it in the light of these verses. He had not crashed onto some foreign shore, a victim of wind and tide. He had been sent by God.

> He had not crashed onto some foreign shore, a victim of wind and tide. He had been sent by God.

Some friends of mine are currently engaged in pastoral ministry in the south of England, but they did not set out with that in mind. They had trained at Bible college with a view to going out to the Far East and had even been accepted by the mission agency, but the health of one of their children made that move impossible. After initially delaying their departure, they eventually came to the reluctant conclusion that they could not go as no long-term improvement in the child's health could be guaranteed. Going into the ministry instead may seem to us, standing on the outside, quite a logical move, but I should think that for them it was one of the most difficult changes in plan they had ever made. All their thoughts had been elsewhere, their hopes and dreams fixed on leaving Britain and telling people they were going, but suddenly they had to reverse their plans. It is not just that life in Britain would seem rather ordinary compared with that in the Far East. Rather, it is that everything God had been saying to them up to that point would have had to be re-appraised: Had they been wrong? Were they letting God down? Was this a mark of failure? I imagine it felt like failure, at least in part. They were going to the wrong part of the world now! But like Paul, they had to come round to see that, even though they were not where they expected to be, they were where God wanted them to be.

You and I are no different. You may look back over the past couple of years in disbelief. You are not where you had hoped or planned to be. In fact, events may have taken such a drastic turn that you feel you are miles from where you should be, in which case you need to take hold of what Paul is saying. You are not at the mercy of fate, driven by chance; God is working out events in your life; you are in his hands; and you are where he wants you now.

> You are not at the mercy of fate, driven by chance.

God has a higher purpose in your troubles

HE IS CONCERNED WITH MORE THAN JUST BLESSING YOU

We are often preoccupied with ourselves and whether God is going to bless us, but God's aims are so much higher than that. If you are ill, for instance, he has something greater than your healing in mind. He may heal you, but that will only be if your healing contributes to the fulfilment of his greater purpose. Or is work stressful? He is concerned with something greater than merely changing your work. Likewise Paul, stuck under house arrest for two years in Rome, did not receive a visit from an angel to spring him out, as Peter had in Acts 12. The Lord had something for him to do from prison that would contribute to his greater purpose.

GOD'S AIM IN EVERYTHING IS TO ADVANCE THE GOSPEL

God's greater purpose is the gospel—the good news—of Jesus Christ, and he therefore shapes our lives so that they will contribute, directly or indirectly, to the spreading of that good news. So it is that Paul writes from prison that 'what has happened to me has really served to advance the gospel' (1:12). Of course, it is at just this point that faith is necessary and will be severely tested. It certainly didn't look as if the gospel was advancing. The number one apostle to the Gentile world was locked away, prevented from preaching where he was in Rome, unable either to visit the churches he had established or go to found new ones, and with nothing more than a very irregular messenger service to keep him in touch. Where is the good in all that? It sounds pretty disastrous for the gospel. Yet in the face of all that Paul still insists that his imprisonment and suffering have led to the advance of the gospel, rather than its retreat.

IN OUR SETBACKS GOD CREATES NEW OPPORTUNITIES FOR THE GOSPEL

Paul can see clearly what God has done through his imprisonment and, while you and I might not be granted such a clear vision of the way God is using our troubles for the gospel, the principles remain the same for us. Firstly, there was the direct influence upon those whose path crossed his: 'As a result, it has become clear throughout the whole palace guard and to everyone else that I am in chains for Christ' (1:13). Everyone around heard the good news about Jesus as Paul took the opportunity to explain the circumstances of his arrest to all who came his way. The most likely targets for his evangelism would have been the soldiers to whom he was permanently chained. Prisoners waiting to see the emperor were closely guarded, with the best way of preventing escape being to chain the prisoner to a guard. Paul did not see himself as their prisoner in this circumstance, but took the opportunity to preach to his captive audience, one by one as they rotated duties. In addition to this they would also have heard him pray, read the Bible (out loud was the custom), receive visitors and dictate his letters. It is hardly surprising that everyone around knew what was going on.

And notice that Paul's rotating congregation was a group of people who, under normal circumstances, would not have come into contact with Christians, except possibly to have seen them die in the arena. Paul was not afraid to go where no one else had been, but even he would have found it difficult to reach the emperor's personal guard and household. Can you imagine him sauntering up to the barracks gate with a pack of literature and requesting permission to visit the troops? Army Scripture readers didn't have representatives in those days and chaplains, if they had had them, would have been pagan, so most people would have concluded that this was an unreached people group that required creative approaches in order to gain access. God's creativity took Paul right in and brought him into contact with just about everybody in the garrison.

But in addition to the effect on Paul's captors, there was the indirect influence on fellow Christians in Rome: 'Because of my chains, most of the brothers in the Lord have been encouraged to speak the word of God more courageously and fearlessly' (1:14). His example was an inspiration to Roman Christians to courageous witness and preaching, which is not quite what you would expect. The natural response to the imprisonment of a leader is for the flock to take cover, keep their heads down and not make trouble, which is just why pastors are always the first target for persecution by authorities. But God has so worked in the lives of these Christians through Paul's suffering that they were stirred to action, so that more people were doing the work than if Paul alone was doing it.

> God has gone ahead of them to bring them to that place and in doing so has created opportunities to share the love of Christ and the message of the gospel that would never otherwise have existed.

Notice that both these effects are specifically ascribed to Paul's suffering: 'As a result …' (of what happened to Paul) and 'Because of my chains …' They happened *because* Paul was in prison and not merely in spite of it. Neither would have taken place in quite the same way if Paul had gained his liberty four years earlier. The gospel had advanced because God had created new openings for the message by sending the messenger where he would not have chosen to go.

Christian history is littered with people who find themselves in similar circumstances. Surprising heroes, unwilling missionaries, unexpected evangelists who are swept overboard in the storms of life and find themselves washed up on the shores of desolation. They end up in the company of people they would naturally shun, in places they would normally avoid, yet discover that God has gone ahead of them to bring them to that place and in doing so has created opportunities to share the love of Christ and the message of the gospel that would never otherwise have existed. The gospel spreads *because* of the setback, not just in spite of it.

Sometimes God takes quite drastic action. Here, in order to reach the emperor, God has sent his apostle in chains. That is drastic indeed, but it may be quite simple in your case: your train is delayed and you commiserate with a fellow traveller, which opens up a conversation about Christ that would not have taken place if the train had been on time.

On a much broader scale, the more recent expulsion of missionaries from China is a perfect example of what Paul says here coming to fruition. After the Communist revolution and takeover in the 1950s missionaries were quickly thrown out, branded as foreign subversives. The Christian world was in turmoil over two questions that arose out of the expulsions. What was going to happen to the church in China, now that it was cut off from the world? And why did God permit so many men and women, whom he had called, to find their work suddenly at an end? The answer to the first question has emerged only in the last ten or fifteen years, in that God has brought about amazing growth in the Chinese church, even though it has endured fearful persecution. The disappearance of outside support was a cue for the awakening of the church. And the second question is answered when you look at where the missionaries went. They were recycled and spread out through the whole of South-East Asia, turning the 'China Inland Mission' into the 'Overseas Missionary Fellowship' with a ministry to growing churches there in a way that might not have happened otherwise. In what at first appeared to be disaster for the cause of Christ, God was basically redeploying his missionary force.

> In what at first appeared to be disaster for the cause of Christ, God was basically redeploying his missionary force.

In all such cases, where something appears to block you, Paul insists that you exercise faith and believe that God will overrule any apparent setback to bring good out of it not only for you, but also for the progress of the gospel. What that means is that you must recalibrate your thinking about 'setbacks' and realize that they are not setbacks at all in God's hands. The event itself becomes a stepping stone for God's purpose.

Learn to look at life from God's perspective

It takes faith to see events in this way. It involves adopting God's outlook and perspective on life, rather than giving way to fatalistic hopelessness. To do that may mean switching off the signals you have been listening to until now and completely retuning your mind to receive what God has to say about your situation. Paul demonstrates one way of doing this as he writes this section, where his whole focus is upon Christ.

IN CHAINS FOR CHRIST (1:14)

There is probably no more succinct way of Paul stating his beliefs about his imprisonment than this. It is not a setback, disaster or even a minor hitch. It is 'for Christ', doing what Jesus wants, and is part of God's will for him. Elsewhere, in Ephesians 3:1, he calls himself a 'prisoner of Christ Jesus', which puts it even more graphically, as if Christ were holding him there.

> The event itself becomes a stepping stone for God's purpose.

When everything goes wrong, it is faith-stretching to think this way, yet it is also faith-strengthening, since it involves reminding yourself that however bad the situation, Jesus Christ is the one who is calling the shots. This attitude could not be more radically different from the despairing frustration that we normally express at the blocking of our plans. Of course, it doesn't give a specific answer to the question of why Jesus might have permitted these circumstances to arise, but it does reassure you that he has brought them about, that he is in control and that you go through them with him and for him.

CHRIST IS PREACHED (1:18)

Here is what counts for Paul. No mention of the discomfort and suffering (although there was plenty of both). What is finally important is that people around were hearing the gospel. Even with some preaching out of false motives, he is nevertheless overjoyed that the benefit of his suffering has been to bring others within the sound of the good news. Go into a hospital ward and you will not hear much rejoicing along these lines. People are usually only too glad to get out and be on the road to recovery to be thinking about whether others are going to be helped by their illness. But a Christian response, which does not exclude the desire to be free from suffering, takes the very hard route of praying that the believer might be a herald of the gospel to those around through that suffering. To do this, you have to realize and accept that your own comfort, security, well-being and even happiness are of secondary importance to this higher purpose.

There are many examples of Christians sent to prison in order to reach the prisoners. A number of years ago a short report in an issue of some Scripture Union Bible notes related the story of a pastor in Guatemala who had managed to become entangled in events around the murder of a man accused of attempting to abduct a child. Quite wrongly, the pastor had been arrested and charged with the man's murder, even though he had actually been pleading with the police to protect the man. The report concluded simply by saying, 'Since he was unjustly locked up in prison, he has led many to Christ.' While not minimizing the pastor's discomfort at being wrongly sent to jail, the report rightly highlighted the favourable effects: many had heard the good news and had been converted.

> It is not a setback, disaster or even a minor hitch. It is 'for Christ'

JESUS CHRIST HONOURED (1:20–21)

Is there a more sublime expression of Paul's fervent hope in Christ than that found in these verses? Everything he endures he does so for Christ, so that his Lord and Saviour is honoured. If he had founded a Christian business enterprise, these verses would have featured in the mission statement and would have been the heart of the corporate logo. As it was, he founded Christian churches and demonstrated by example what we are here for, what undergirds all our aims and what forms the basis of our hope. In life or death, we live to glorify Jesus. Living or dying; joy or sorrow; success or failure; all present opportunities to lift up Jesus Christ before a watching world. And in the final analysis, it does not matter which of these God sends us. To live is Christ; to die is gain. Will you have that as a motto over all of your life's transactions?

CONDUCT WORTHY OF CHRIST (1:27)

Note the 'Whatever'. In every eventuality conduct yourself in a way that demonstrates the hope you have in Jesus Christ—which means that you must see every eventuality as an opportunity. Make sure there is something of Christ in your present difficulties. Don't make the mistake of thinking that you will only be able to serve Jesus Christ if matters improve. You can honour him now. Don't give way to bitterness or self-pity. Remember that the Lord has brought you to the place you are at now and is with you still, so let your conduct and speech reflect that. You may not be able to say to friends why something has happened, but you will at least be able to say, 'We are trusting that the Lord will continue to help us', and show that by the way you live.

This is not an easy option

Far from being easy, this is the hardest route to take. There is still going to be an element that you will not be able to understand. God does not provide you with answers to every dilemma. When the seventeenth-century Puritan minister John Flavel wrote a book on the way God orders our lives he entitled it *The Mystery of Providence* and every other book on the subject since then is in some way indebted to that title. There is an element of mystery to living by faith that makes faith absolutely necessary. You will not be able to see forward very far because God does not provide light for the whole of your route ahead, as if following him is like driving on well-lit motorways. God has called you to follow him down the country lanes, where the potholes are large and where you will frequently be on your own, and the light he provides will be just enough for the path before your feet.

But there is immense reassurance to be drawn from the way Paul writes, even if you can't explain it to others. If the stuffing has been knocked out of you, and your hopes, plans and dreams lie in tatters, then Paul's words contain enough substance to hold you up. The mystery of providence is at the same time a source of undying comfort. Belief in God's providence does not require you to understand what God is doing at all times. It does not exclude the possibility of your being completely at a loss to know why something has happened. But it tells you God is doing *something* and that he has not left you high and dry. Paul's words assure you that God is working behind the scenes, directing events with an unseen hand and infinite wisdom. If disaster has struck, you have the promise that God will nevertheless bring out of that disaster something which glorifies him, which will take the gospel forward, and which will be to your strengthening too.

Summary: Setbacks are stepping stones for God's purpose.

Key verse: Philippians 1:12: 'What has happened to me has really served to advance the gospel.'

To think about: Looking back over my life, are there painful events I need to look at in a different light and believe that God was in fact at work in them?

'You intended to harm me, but God intended it for good', Genesis 50:20.

'[God] works out everything in conformity with the purpose of his will', Ephesians 1:11.

'With the help of our God we dared to tell you his gospel in spite of strong opposition', 1 Thessalonians 2:2.

Thinking more deeply

The mystery of providence defies our attempt to tame it by reason. I do not mean it is illogical; I mean that we do not know enough to be able to unpack it and domesticate it. Perhaps we may gauge how content we are to live with our limitations by assessing whether we are comfortable in joining the biblical writers in utterances that mock our frankly idolatrous devotion to our own capacity to understand. Are we embarrassed, for instance, by the prophetic rebuke to the clay that wants to tell the potter how to set about his work (Isaiah 29:16; 45:9)?

Don Carson, *How long, O Lord?*

The heathen Roman emperors, who made the world tremble and subdued nations under them, employed all their power and policy against the poor, naked, defenceless church, to ruin it, yet could not accomplish it … yet the church lives … [By contrast] how successful have weak and contemptible means been made for the good of the church! Thus in the first planting of the church in the world, by what weak and improbable instruments was it done! Christ did not choose the eloquent orators, or men of authority in the courts of kings and emperors, but twelve poor artisans and fishermen; and these not sent together in a troop, but some to take one country to conquer it, and some another. The most ridiculous course, in appearance, for such a design as could be imagined, and yet in how short a time was the gospel spread and the churches planted by them in the several kingdoms of the world!

John Flavel, *The Mystery of Providence.*

Note

1 Look, for instance, at verses 16 and 29.

My story

Delayed answers

This account of the trials of a converted animist in Burkina Faso (formerly Upper Volta) is related by Brian Woodford, a former missionary with WEC International. It is a good example of the many ways in which God's people are tested, but reveals that God brings fruit from it all in the end.

One morning in 1939 a fair-haired Irish missionary named Charles Benington drove in his Model A Ford into a remote tribal village in Upper Volta. Malba was one of the villages of the Birifor tribe, which numbered about 40,000 people, most of whom were under the control of a chief named Bompitay. Benington went to this chief to ask if he would gather the people that evening so that he could address them.

A crowd of men assembled that evening and listened to the story of the Creator God who made the heavens and the earth and called on people to worship him alone. Benington spoke the language of the neighbouring Lobi tribe, but most Birifors understood this, so when he made an appeal for anyone who was prepared to put his faith in the Living God, two brothers stood up. One was a man called Samba, one of the chief's henchmen and his head drummer. Samba took Benington back with him to his house to talk into the night and, there under the stars, Samba prayed to this Living God whose name was Jesus. Benington wrote in his diary the next morning that when Samba prayed on that flat mud roof it was so real that it was as if he could hear the angels singing up in heaven.

After Benington left, the chief called in the two men and congratulated them for 'putting on a good show for the white man' and told them to forget all about it. Samba's brother had kept his idols hidden in his shoulder bag, so he turned back to them without hesitation, but Samba refused. He had already destroyed all his idols.

Consequently Samba fell out of favour with the chief and lost his job. He had two wives, but the difficulties that came from his faith resulted in one dying and the other running away, so he was left to bring up his small daughter alone. The chief even tried to starve him to death. No one would help him cultivate, or give him any food. One time Samba was tied up and left to die on an anthill, but his little girl found him and cut the ropes. But when she was old enough the chief took her as a wife (he had dozens already), and eventually a little boy was born to them.

Samba waited for someone to come and teach him more, but no one came. A few times Benington came back and prayed with him and each time, after he had gone, the chief had Samba beaten. After waiting over four years Samba began to pray that God would send a teacher so he could learn how to share his faith with his own people. He only knew that there was a Living God who created the world and that his name was Jesus, and therefore he could have no other gods or idols. When he died he knew he would go to God's country, and his ambition was to sit on a stool next to Benington.

When I was ten I was confined to bed with mumps. My mother bought me Joyce Reason's children's book of the life of David Livingstone. I read it through and was fascinated by the pictures of Livingstone being attacked by a lion and setting slaves free from the Arab slave traders. I prayed, 'O God, I would like to be a missionary in Africa like David Livingstone.' Immediately a reply came into my head. 'All right, then you shall be.' It was a silent voice but very specific. Words I have never forgotten.

Years later, while at the WEC Missionary Training College in Glasgow I listened to a missionary home from Upper Volta tell about a man who lived alone, the only believer in his tribe, who had been waiting for years for someone to come and tell him more. I knew that was my call. I arrived in 1960 and discovered Samba, still waiting. He lived alone in a mud house that had so fallen down he had not even room to stretch out his sleep mat. Snakes and rats shared the mud ruin.

When I learnt enough of the language to talk with him Samba shared his story. I counted back and figured that the year Samba first prayed for God to send a missionary was the very year I was in bed with mumps and heard God's voice. But it took sixteen years for Samba to see the answer to his prayer. He had not stopped praying, or trusting in this invisible God. Samba was a true Abraham, standing firm on the little bit of revelation he had received, knowing there was more to discover.

I went to visit the old chief, Bompitay, surrounded by his idols (and his fifty wives and two hundred children). I asked permission to come and live in his village and tell the people about Jesus who was the Living Creator God, but he refused. He had enough gods, he told me, and he didn't want Jesus. So I had to leave, and pray that God would open the door. Four months later the chief fell out with the French colonial authorities and a pitched battle ensued. All the wives and children were scattered (including Samba's daughter and grandson), while Bompitay escaped on a bicycle to Ghana and never came back.

So the way opened and I found a three-roomed mud house with a tin roof and moved in, with Samba. We eventually rediscovered his two year old grandson, and he came to live with us. This was my life from 1960 to 1971. A church was planted, the Birifor language reduced to written form, and leaders trained. I eventually went back to complete the translation of the New Testament, and the church now thrives under Birifor leadership with no missionary presence. Samba went home to glory in 1970. Daniel, his grandson, is a pastor and has been Principal of the Hebron Pastoral Institute in Ivory Coast. At the time of writing he is in the last stages of presenting his PhD dissertation (in French) on the training of church leadership in the African context.

6 Waiting:
According to plan

Learning patience when life grinds to a halt

To wait in his place, and to go at his pace (John Piper, Future Grace).

Please read Genesis 39–40.

It is a feature of the animal kingdom that the closer a creature is to the ground the more limited its horizon is. Thus a mouse sees only what is immediately around it and relies on hearing and smell to alert it to danger it cannot see. The kestrel, which hunts it, hovers above the ground and literally has a bird's-eye view of all the terrain around and of anything that moves on the ground beneath it. The mouse's world is restricted; the kestrel's, expansive and broad.

> Under pressure of setback and misfortune we easily succumb to the notion that God has forgotten about us.

It would be fair to say that our view of the world in spiritual terms is more like the mouse's than that of the kestrel. We are so close to the ground that our view of the horizon is pitifully limited. Nowhere is this more evident than in our understanding (or rather, lack of it) of what God is doing in our lives. Under pressure of setback and misfortune we easily succumb to the notion that God has forgotten about us, abandoned us, or is even punishing us for some sin we imagine we have committed against him. The trials we endure blur our vision, hiding the hand of God, making our present distresses a bad place from which to see what God is doing. We are so near to the ground that we can see nothing but the trouble that is swooping down on us and which threatens to carry us off. We need a higher perspective, or at least something to indicate that the higher perspective exists at all.

Signposts

The story of Joseph is bracketed by indications that his life is not randomly ordered or out of control, but that God is directing it. At both the beginning and end of the account there are details which stand out like signposts announcing the involvement of God. Like beacons they shine in the darkness as a reminder that God is present all the way through.

At the beginning of the account, in chapter 37, Joseph reports a couple of dreams to his family. Dreams feature on several occasions in the story and each dream is of vital importance for the direction of events. However, Joseph's dreams were not well received by his family—it was possibly the way he told them—and only fuelled the hatred his brothers had for him, precipitating the events that led to them selling him into slavery. Yet the dreams at the beginning of the story came from God. God spoke through them, even though his family did not recognize this, indicating that Joseph would achieve prominence, although he did not give any details about how this would come about (which was just as well!), nor why it was to happen.

> The story of Joseph is bracketed by indications that his life is not randomly ordered or out of control, but that God is directing it.

At the end of the story, in chapter 50, Joseph looks back and, from the higher perspective of hindsight, is able to acknowledge that God did lead him all the way. The opportunity to express this arises when his brothers come to him and, in an indirect manner, ask him to forgive them and not hold their crimes against them. His reply is one that beautifully summarizes the mysterious combination of human sinfulness and God's perfect plan for you and me: 'You intended to harm me, but God intended it for good' (Genesis 50:20). Even the brothers' violent aggression was not beyond the reach of God. God used it to take Joseph to Egypt in order to prepare a way for the saving of Joseph's family. It is important for us to realize that Joseph is saying that, in all the suffering he endured, God was there with him. With that suffering over, he looks back and tells us that God did not leave him to rot, but planned it so that even the very worst features were used for good.

The writer is signalling to us that God is directing events throughout. At the beginning he announces what is to come, albeit in cryptic terms for Joseph. At the end he reviews the past and says God was there all the time. God did not abandon Joseph to his fate, nor stand idly by, watching the drama unfold. We have to admit that, more often than not, we visualize God as little more than an extra in the play, when the story of Joseph should make us see that he is the writer, producer and director, and the leading actor, too. He is intimately involved in leading us to the denouement he has planned. In Joseph's case he took the brothers' hatred and put it to good effect; he sent him to jail and blessed him there; he used contacts gained from that to make Joseph Prime Minister, promoting him to the position of prominence his dreams predicted; and thus he put him in the only place from which he would be able to save his family from starvation.

> We visualize God as little more than an extra in the play, when the story of Joseph should make us see that he is the writer, producer and director, and the leading actor, too.

The signposts are there for us, since Joseph would not have been able to see them both until the end of his life. It is quite likely that Joseph would not have understood much of God's aims at the time in the suffering he endured. If he had thought he grasped what God was saying to him in the dreams he was given as a teenager, one can imagine the deep confusion he must have felt at being sold into slavery and then thrown into prison. And, of course, we are no different. In the deepest darkness we begin to doubt God and wonder if we are in a chapter that he didn't write. Or we feel that perhaps he has simply written us out of his story so that, like some TV soap character who disappears from the screen, we will never feature in God's plan again. But the signposts that the writer has erected tell us otherwise. They stand clear above the surrounding terrain that makes it so difficult for us to see what God is doing, and announce that he is there from beginning to end frequently invisible, yes, but never absent, and always in control.

At snail's pace?

The signposts are necessary because there are two areas in which it frequently looks as if God has lost his way. The first of these concerns the speed at which he works; the second, the route he takes to fulfil his plans.

We must never forget that God is not in a hurry. However, when viewed from the human perspective it does often appear that God is taking a dreadfully long time over everything. We easily become frustrated at any apparent lack of progress, wanting immediate action and even becoming desperate if we do not seem to get it. Paul experienced this and it is even more evident in the life of Abraham. One of the repeated cries of the Scriptures is 'How long, O Lord?'

Be merciful to me, LORD, for I am faint;
   O LORD, heal me, for my bones are in agony.
My soul is in anguish.
   How long, O LORD, how long?
(Psalm 6:2–3)

This example expresses the despair of wondering why an illness continues for such a great length of time, but the other psalms have wider concerns than illness (such as bringing about justice), situations in which God does not appear to be taking action when we think he should.

> We must never forget that God is not in a hurry.

How long was Joseph in the waiting room? The account does not leave us guessing, since it tells us that he was 'a young man of seventeen' when he ratted on his brothers and earned their hatred (Genesis 37:2), and that he was thirty years old when he was finally made Prime Minister (Genesis 41:46). Thirteen years in slavery and prison! And that was followed by another nine before he encountered his family again. That feels like the most appalling delay and gives poignancy to the account when it passes over some of those years with the simple phrase 'Some time later' (Genesis 40:1).

We measure time in seconds and minutes, counting delays in hours as terrible ('My train was over two hours late,' we complain bitterly. 'What a waste of time!'). We measure recovery from illness in weeks and months, since we grudgingly acknowledge that the process of convalescence is slower. But God is quite capable of measuring time for the progress he desires in years.

Look at the end of Genesis 40. Joseph interpreted a dream for Pharaoh's cupbearer which came true and saw the man restored to his former position in Pharaoh's household. Thinking that the man would remember the favourable outcome of the dream and the help he had given, Joseph instructed the cupbearer to appeal to Pharaoh on his behalf when he was released. But the chapter ends with the revelation that the cupbearer simply forgot Joseph on his release, and the following chapter begins, 'When two full years had passed …' God may use a calendar to measure time, instead of a clock (rather like some preachers are accused of doing), and we had better get used to it.

God is quite capable of measuring time for the progress he desires in years.

The book of Genesis contains another breathtaking example of a time warp that takes place as we move from one chapter to the next. The background this time is that in Genesis 15 Abraham had been promised a son of his own through whom his line would continue, but after years of trying he and Sarah still had no children. So they took matters into their own hands; in chapter 16 they reasoned that, since Sarah was well past childbearing age, God must have intended them to have a son via Sarah's maidservant, Hagar. She was younger and obviously more fertile, and the custom of the day allowed this expedient for childless couples. Hagar would have the child for them and they would adopt the child as their own—and since it would be Abraham's child and Sarah's stepchild, that would be enough for it to be the heir. Perfect. Except that God did not intend it to happen this way.

This first-recorded instance of surrogate motherhood is a sad example of the logic of human reasoning taking over from the logic of faith. Human reason argues that the delay must mean God has another way and sets about finding it, creating trouble in the process (to see what trouble Abraham and Sarah caused, read the chapter to see the terrible jealousy that came over Sarah when the child was born and the mean way Sarah treated Hagar and her son—and then look at the world situation now, at the current conflict between the descendants of Ishmael and Isaac, that is, between Arab and Israeli). Of course, it is quite possible that God has another way when answers are delayed, but Abraham and Sarah should have taken time to hear what God was saying in the delay, rather than jumping to the first idea that suggested itself to them. The logic of faith listens to God and, on hearing him say 'Wait', does just that.

It appears that Abraham learnt his lesson—and here is the time warp in the text. Chapter 16 ends with the remark that Abraham was eighty-six when Ishmael was born. The next chapter opens with the words, 'When Abraham was ninety-nine years old ...' It is quite easy to miss what this meant for Abraham, since most of us do not often read across the chapter divisions. These divisions are not part of the original text, but were inserted to help us find passages more easily, but in this case the result of their presence is that we fail to notice that after Ishmael's birth—which in itself was about eleven years after Abraham had left his home in Ur—Abraham had to wait another thirteen years before God communicated the next stage of the plan. Those years are unrecorded and pass unnoticed from one sentence to the next. As with Joseph, we can be certain that God had not absented himself from the story during this period, but it must nevertheless go down as the silent years in the waiting room.

> The waiting room is one of the most difficult places to be in because we are so obviously not in control.

The waiting room is one of the most difficult places to be in because we are so obviously not in control. We are waiting for something to happen over which we have no power, and are therefore completely dependent upon someone else. When this powerlessness combines with an apparent delay on this someone else's part in coming to our assistance, and when we know he possesses every ability to help us, we become impatient, frustrated and fretful. John Piper has a helpful observation about such impatience and what we ought to be aiming for:

Impatience is a form of unbelief. It's what we begin to feel when we start to doubt the wisdom of God's timing or the goodness of his guidance. It springs up in our hearts when our plan is interrupted or shattered. It may be prompted by a long wait in a checkout line or a sudden blow that knocks out half our dreams. The opposite of impatience is not a glib denial of loss. It's a deepening, ripening, peaceful willingness to *wait for* God in the *unplanned place* of obedience, and to *walk with* God at the *unplanned pace* of obedience—to wait in his place, and to go at his pace.[1]

Impatience is one of the ugliest characteristics that we can display, but we tend to think little of it because it seems of no consequence. Yet we should take it more seriously, because other, more damaging, traits travel in its wake. Impatience may be accompanied by (among other things) doubts about God, rebellious unbelief about what he intends for us, a self-centredness that demands things work out our way, a bitter hostility to others who are not in the same situation, a cynicism about the fairness of life, self pity … The list could go on and it would not make for happy reading.

By contrast patience (literally 'longsuffering', as it appears in the older translations of the Bible) is one of the key—and most beautiful—attributes of mature faith. This 'deepening, ripening, peaceful willingness' is something really worth striving for. In the letter to the Hebrews, the writer expresses the desire that his readers might not drift from their secure moorings in Christ, but instead 'through faith and patience' they might inherit what has been promised (6:12). Significantly, the example he then chooses to illustrate his point is Abraham and his long wait for the fulfilment of the promise that he and Sarah would have a child of their own. Waiting patiently was what Abraham did for around twenty-five years. Since the Bible tells us that we are his children in the faith and God wants us to mature in that faith as Abraham did, we can expect to have to do the same.

Taking the scenic route

Delay is just one aspect of the problem Joseph faced. Diversion is the other.

It is one thing to believe you know where God is taking you (and not all of us do). It is quite another to say you know the actual route he is going to take to reach this destination. It appears that Joseph understood enough from his dreams to be able to say that God was going to put him in a position of great prominence, so great that even his family would bow down to him. It was, after all, his relating of this that so riled his brothers that they sold him into slavery—they understood all too clearly what was going to happen and voted against it. But Joseph was not able to say how God would get him there, nor could he have had any idea of what would be the personal cost involved in attaining such prominence.

Joseph discovered that God frequently takes the most roundabout route to reach his goal and it will be quite different to the one you would naturally choose for yourself. There will be many detours and diversions, bypaths and minor trails, apparently blocked roads, accidents, rough tracks and potholes, which translate into setbacks and disasters, years out of circulation, catastrophic mistakes and failures, misunderstandings and apparent changes of plan. There may be years in which you feel you are doing nothing but going around in circles, stuck in what appears to be a pointless round from which you are unable to escape. Joseph cannot have remained immune from feeling that way in prison. His words in Genesis 40:14–15 betray a sense of despair at being locked away for so long. From our perspective we can see that God had not left him alone in prison while he went away for a few years to attend to someone else. He was with Joseph all the time, taking him the way he wanted, and you must believe that he is doing the same with you.

> Joseph discovered that God frequently takes the most roundabout route to reach his goal and it will be quite different to the one you would naturally choose for yourself.

This has some important applications for us today in the matter of the training of Christian workers. We frequently imagine that God's only purpose is to make a man or woman into, say, a missionary, and to do so in the most efficient way possible. So he calls the person, sends him or her to Bible college for three years and there you are! One mature missionary!

But that's not the way it is. Instead of going straight from A to B— volunteer to missionary via the fast track training programme—there is a whole host of apparently unrelated difficulties, minor irritations, frustrations and irrelevant distractions to endure, all seemingly unconnected with training for the job. And once on the job it is no different. Whether minister or missionary, Christian workers seem to be encumbered with duties and responsibilities that have no link with 'the real work' they are supposed to be doing, but that is because God has more in mind than making a person into something. His plan involves more than you merely reaching a goal: it involves what you do while getting there.

The difference between these two methods is perhaps best described by thinking of the way in which twenty-first century missionary travel differs from how people travelled just fifty years ago. Today, cheap air flights have changed the way people think about travel. Arriving is what counts and the journey is to be as quick and direct as possible. But fifty years ago, the travelling was part of the enjoyment, an integrated part of the process. So missionaries didn't roar around the world in aircraft; they booked a place on a ship, sat back and enjoyed the trip. With sometimes several weeks on board while the ship crossed oceans and called in at numerous other ports, the journey became the last phase of training. It gave time to put the home country behind and prepare for the new challenge ahead. In that time, today's short-term mission teams will have already built a hospital wing, done three evangelistic crusades and given a presentation to their home church on their return.

> God has booked you a place on the slow boat that winds its tortuous way through the islands of experience, with the intention that you learn en route.

The contrast between the two modes of transport could not be more apt. Air travel: quick, efficient, direct. Sea travel: meandering, tedious, slow. You don't need me to tell you which one is a better description of the way God trains not just missionaries or ministers, but all of his children. God has booked you a place on the slow boat that winds its tortuous way through the islands of experience, with the intention that you learn en route (and, moreover, he is not worried if it takes years to achieve it). Helen Roseveare, a missionary in the Congo in the 1960s, once addressed a meeting in which she described this process. 'When I first went to Africa I thought he was sending me there to make me into a missionary,' she said. 'I now realize that he sent me in order to make me holy.' You can read her autobiographical books (*Give me this mountain*, for instance) to see that she is talking about the slow boat method of growth.

You can see plenty of characters in the Bible's accounts who found themselves taking the scenic route. After bursting onto the scene following his conversion, Paul then spent years in obscurity before starting his real work and departing on his now famous missionary journeys. What was he doing in Arabia? And all those years shut away in Tarsus? We can say little definite about that period, but we do know that it was not irrelevant or wasted and that it was part of his formation as an apostle of the good news. And what about Joseph? We have already seen how his route to becoming first minister of Egypt was anything but direct. Sold into slavery, falsely accused, thrown into prison—all this took place before he explained Pharaoh's dream, won his freedom and found himself in the position God had intended for him.

John Bunyan was equally certain about this when he wrote *Pilgrim's Progress* as a description of the Christian life. Christian's path twists and winds its way through one apparent diversion after another, so that on many occasions he loses sight of the Celestial City altogether. Hannah Hurnard wrote a similar allegory called *Hinds' Feet on High Places* in which her heroine is allowed to see her goal in the distance and is then told to take a path that leads her directly away from it. Only much later does she discover that the path turns towards the heavenly goal.

One of the dangers of reading Christian biographies is that it is possible to gain the impression that God's greats somehow avoided this rather boring training ground. Didn't missionaries to West Africa in the nineteenth century take their belongings in a coffin because they knew how little time they had? Eighteen months was the average length of service in those days—and you didn't come home for a debrief after that, unless you count being with the Lord as the ultimate debrief. And didn't people like Henry Martyn expend their short lives and accomplish unbelievable feats in just a few years? Martyn's achievements in translating the Scriptures into Persian, among other languages, before his death at the age of 31 are almost without equal. But do not let that fool you into thinking that this is the norm. We are very good at idolizing others and thinking that they are above the normal troubles of life because they are so great. In fact, if they are great at all, it is because they have gone through the normal troubles, not avoided them.

William Carey, seen as the father of the modern mission movement from Britain, perhaps demonstrates this best of all. His whole life seemed to be nothing but delay and diversion, whether it was the length of time it took him to get out to India in the first place, facing troubles with his wife when there (she was slowly going mad), dealing with misunderstandings from the churches who sent him (a letter took months to reach home), having to raise money by working for an indigo company, waiting for his first Hindu convert (eight years) or losing several years' translation work and literature in a fire. At the end of his life he commented that he did not feel himself to be highly gifted, but at least he could plod. And that is exactly the point. He did so much because he took it slowly and accepted the direction in which God led him. His faith was stronger at the end and the list of his achievements is simply breathtaking.

GOD DOES NOT OWE YOU ANY EXPLANATIONS

There is a little question that is rattling around in my head as I write. It is just one little word, but in actual fact is such a big question that we are not going to get an answer. The question is simply, 'Why?'—a little question that causes anguish out of all proportion to its size. It can eat away at the vitals of faith if you are not careful and can completely undermine confidence in God, because in the end it demands that God explain himself to you. It is as if you are saying, yes, God does know what he is doing; yes, he does understand the issue infinitely more clearly than I do; yes, he can both see the future and control it, while I can only aim and hope; and this ought to be enough, but somehow I still would like him to let me know what he is doing and why. Won't he give me an outline plan of the route he is taking and the timetable he is working to? The brief answer is, No.

The experience of Joseph is that God does not provide such details, at least not to the extent that you might desire. You are promised enough to let you know where you should be going when you need to know it, but that knowledge does not provide an itinerary for the whole of the journey like some celestial bus tour with its details of coffee stops and museum visits. Take Abraham as another example. He received nothing more than the following instructions: 'Leave your country, your people and your father's household and go to the land I will show you' (Genesis 12:1). The New Testament clarifies what that actually meant for him, informing us that he 'obeyed and went, even though he did not know where he was going' (Hebrews 11:8). So he left Ur with nothing more than a series of promises that God gave to him, but he did not know which was to be his land until he actually arrived and God said to him that this was the place. And even then, we know that he did not receive it himself; it was promised to his as yet unborn offspring.

In addition to God not mapping out the future, it is also important to recognize that there will be many unexplained features about the past. Maps have a box in one corner marked 'Legend' which enables us to interpret the map and every feature on it, but God does not do that for everything we pass through. He does not necessarily provide a key to understanding what has happened. God does not usually give the mouse the view that the kestrel has. Take Joseph again, for instance. We have noted that he was able to look back at the end of his life and see what God had done overall, but we are given no explanation for many of the individual events that took place within that period.

Look again at his period of imprisonment and the incident with the cupbearer in Genesis 40. It was perfectly reasonable for Joseph to ask the cupbearer to put in a good word for him with the king. Faced with the same situation we would reason that God had sent him and that this was his way of facilitating release from prison. So why did this man then forget Joseph for two years? Which is another way of asking, Why did *God* let him forget for two years? It isn't enough to say that Pharaoh's dreams came two years later and that if Joseph had got out of prison in chapter 40 he wouldn't have been in Egypt in chapter 41 to interpret the dreams and become Prime Minister, so the family (with Joseph) would have starved to death in chapter 42. That is true as far as it goes, but is not good enough, because it was *God* who sent the dreams. Why did God wait two more years before he gave those dreams to Pharaoh and thus jogged the memory of the absent-minded cupbearer? Why not two weeks?

There is no answer to that question.

Plenty of interesting theories have arisen about Joseph needing to learn to let God do things at his speed and not try to wangle his way out of a tricky situation before God wanted him out; but they are spiritually-minded guesses at best. No reason for the delay is given. And neither does Joseph attempt an explanation later. He acknowledges that God was directing events, but does not answer why events took the direction they did.

This is because God does not give account of all his actions to us. Read the end of the book of Job and you will see that. God finally speaks to Job about the complaints he (that is, Job) had been making about his troubles, but God does not explain his actions. So you may find yourself unable to fathom God's intentions and aims and the nagging question 'Why?' goes unanswered. Why that car accident? Why did I lose my job? Why is the church in such turmoil? Why are my children in trouble? Why does God move so painfully slowly? There is a poignant incident in *The Last Battle*, the final story of C.S. Lewis's *Narnia* chronicles. A rather slow-minded bear has joined Tirian, the last king of Narnia, after initially being fooled by Shift the ape's deception (he had dressed Puzzle the donkey up to look like the lion, Aslan). In the first skirmish the bear is mortally wounded and dies with a bewildered look on its face and the words 'I don't understand' on its lips.

> He acknowledges that God was directing events, but does not answer why events took the direction they did.

Yet being without an answer is not the same as being without God. God has a direction to all that he does. He knows where he is going, even if you do not. He is in control of the plan and your problem may simply be that you are finding it hard to understand what is going on. You should not let that shake your confidence that God knows and that he has not left you.

GOD IS TRUSTWORTHY, BUT UNFATHOMABLE

Never forget it is God you are dealing with. In the end, it is this that satisfied Job. He had no answers to his questions, but he still had God.

So too with Joseph. Joseph's story demonstrates that God is trustworthy.

God had a plan and he stuck to it. He did not lose his way and only get back on it after rediscovering the map. Nor did he lose Joseph for thirteen years. He was leading Joseph all the time. But if you see again that God is trustworthy, you will also appreciate from the account that he is unfathomable.

Here is one of the clear differences between us and Christ. Jesus understood his Father's will perfectly, when all around him misunderstood. In the wake of the prophetic movements of the late 1980s and early 1990s claims have been made that we can know God's mind flawlessly and have exactly the same discernment as Jesus, but in reality it is foolish for people to think like this. Isaiah tells us that God's ways are higher than ours, his thoughts beyond our reach, and the fact that we have moved from the Old Testament to the New does not change that fundamental truth. It *is* possible to have a knowledge of God and his will for you (something which needs to be affirmed in the face of those today who insist God cannot be known at all), but it is altogether another thing to say you know, or can know, *everything* God has for you. You cannot. Paul says of us that 'we see but a poor reflection as in a mirror' (1 Corinthians 13:12), and of God that 'his paths [are] beyond tracing out' (Romans 11:33). Your knowledge of God and his will is limited and finite, and is going to remain that way.

> Yet being without an answer is not the same as being without God.

Fortunately, however, you and I are not called to understand everything perfectly. We are simply called to know, trust and follow the one who does.

Summary: God is not in a hurry.

Key verses: Hebrews 6:12,15: 'We do not want you to become lazy, but to imitate those who through faith and patience inherit what has been promised … And so after waiting patiently, Abraham received what was promised.'

To think about: In what ways have I been impatient with God because he has not done what I think he should have done? How do I need to change my attitude?

'Wait for the Lord; be strong and take heart and wait for the Lord', Psalm 27:14.

'I waited patiently for the LORD; he turned to me and heard my cry. He lifted me out of the slimy pit, out of the mud and mire; he set my feet on a rock and gave me a firm place to stand', Psalm 40:1–2.

'If we hope for what we do not yet have, we wait for it patiently', Romans 8:25.

Thinking more deeply

The climb [to the summit of Mount Sherman in Colorado], as I reflected on it later, recapitulated what I have learned about the pilgrimage of faith. It involves miscalculation, thrills and hardship, long periods of waiting and long periods of simply trudging. No matter how thoroughly I prepare, make precautions, and try to eliminate risk, I never succeed. Always there are times of whiteout, when I can see nothing and avalanches roar down around me. When I reach the summit, though, nothing in the world compares to that feeling of accomplishment and exaltation.

Philip Yancey, *Reaching for the Invisible God.*

Note

1 **John Piper,** *Future Grace* (Leicester: IVP, 1995), p. 171 (my emphasis).

My story

God is not in a hurry

W.B. Forsyth worked as a missionary in Brazil from 1928 to 1974, serving in many locations across the country. Here he relates how two incidents in his early years bore unexpected fruit many years later.

God's word is not chained

When my first wife, Edith, and I began working in Brazil in the late 1920s there were many towns in which there was no gospel witness. One of these was the town of P. which had been established by a German factory owner. He had constructed a town—without a church of any sort—around his factory, so virtually owned and controlled the whole place, but we and a couple of our colleagues decided that we should make some attempt to preach the gospel there. We were not certain that we would be welcome, but decided to go nevertheless since we had around a thousand copies of the four Gospels to use.

So the four of us turned up early one morning with these Gospels which we began to distribute to the people present. Very quickly a crowd appeared and began to take the literature from us eagerly, but this did not last long. The police arrived, prevented us from handing out the Gospels and arrested us. They took us back to the police compound where we sat for much of the day, with the remaining Gospels in a heap in the dirt. Moreover, throughout the day, it became apparent that the police were confiscating the ones we had succeeding in giving out, because the pile grew as the day wore on. In the end it looked as if the majority of the Gospels had been taken back, but we were not allowed to keep them. We were sent away, without being charged, and without our Gospels too. It appeared to have been a wasted day.

Several years later, I was pastoring a church in the interior (a long way from P.) and was called to the bedside of a poor, dying man. He had never been to our church and I did not know him, but he was clear that he wanted a pastor. As I spoke and prayed with him I realized that he was, in fact, a

Christian, seeking final comfort as he died, and then I noticed something by his bedside that made me miss a heartbeat. By his bed were four copies of the Gospels we had handed out that day! When I asked him how he came by them, he told his story. He told me he had been a worker in the factory in P. when one day some foreigners turned up out of the blue and began to hand out books. He did not know what the books were, but was happy to receive a free gift. He then realized that there were others in the set, so he had come back for more, but when he had all four the police turned up, arrested the missionaries and had then tried to confiscate the books. He had been approached by a policeman who had demanded the books, but he refused to surrender them. Eventually, the policeman, realizing that he had no actual right to take the books, had given up and the man was able to keep his prize. He took them home, read them and in the course of time came to faith through them. Later he had moved from P. to the town where I was working. He died in full assurance of faith.

A number of years after this, I was in another part of Brazil, taking part in an inter-church meeting. There were several testimonies, one of which came from a policeman, standing there in his shining dress uniform. He said that he was on duty one morning in the town of P.—you know where this is going, don't you?—when a carload of foreigners arrived, who then began to hand out literature. The police were ordered by the boss to arrest the foreigners and confiscate the literature, which they did. At the end of the day they sent the foreigners away, but the question arose as to what should happen with the books they had brought? There was some discussion, but burning them was not an option they entertained. The police chief then hit upon the idea of letting each of the policemen take a complete set home, so this man also received a copy of each of the four Gospels. He had read them and had found Christ through them and was testifying to salvation and a changed life.

Quite a few years after this (we are now talking at least twenty years down the line) I was working in another town in the interior where there was an important railway station. At this station, the single track railroad became two tracks so that trains going in opposite directions could cross each day, so it was obviously an important part of the day when this took place. One of my colleagues would use this opportunity to walk down both of the trains as they stood in the station for about an hour and offer tracts and Bibles. One day he returned from the station in a great state of excitement and told me about one of his conversations with a passenger.

He had offered Scriptures but had been rebuffed by a man who had told him that he did not need copies of the Bible because he had enough in his house. Upon being questioned further, the man revealed that he was not a believer but had been the police chief in the town of P. One morning the town had been thrown into chaos by the arrival of a group of foreign missionaries, whom they had arrested. They had confiscated their literature and sent them away, but had not been sure what to do with the books. He had therefore authorized that a set of four should be given to each officer, but there were still several hundred left, so he had taken them to his own house. They were not just sitting there, however. Whenever any dignitary came to the town he ensured that each visitor received a set of the four books as a present, so much so that he now had only a few copies left.

And we thought that this had been a wasted day and that the Gospels had not been distributed!

We never know what God is doing behind the scenes

On another occasion, Edith and I went with some colleagues to do some street preaching in a town where the gospel had not been well-received in the past. It was to prove no different in our case.

We arrived and set up in front of a building on the main street. I was preaching and my wife was playing a small harmonium which we always took with us, while a couple of other missionaries were assisting, but we did not have much of an opportunity to run the meeting. A hostile crowd soon gathered, paid for by the local priest who resented our interference in what he saw as his patch, and it was not long before the rocks began to fly. Although we tried to continue, we quickly realized that we were not going to be able to do so without injury, but escape was not going to be easy, either. The rabble in front of us looked bent on violence, so we were forced to flee the hail of missiles by climbing into the building behind us—through a window—and make a run for it out of the back. Another fruitless expedition?

Over forty years later, at the end of my time in Brazil, I was due to take one last meeting before boarding the ship home. As I was speaking, a man came in late—nothing surprising about that in Brazil!—and sat down at the front of the congregation. All during the meeting he looked at me very intently, as if he was trying to recognize me, and at the end he approached me and introduced himself to me.

He first of all ascertained that I had been in the town I mentioned earlier, then said he had been in the crowd. He had been one of those paid by the priest to break up the meeting and had taken his place among the stone throwers. But the experience had unnerved him in an unexpected way. Even as he was throwing stones a couple of questions had occurred to him: Why would these people come here and take all this? What was so special about the message that they would risk injury to get it across? He did not have the answers to those questions, but set himself to finding out. His journey eventually led him to a personal faith in the Lord Jesus Christ and, hearing that I was speaking at a church near to where he now lived, he had come to tell me that our interrupted service had not been in vain.

7 Disappointment:
Not what I had been led to expect

Surviving the feeling that God has failed you

It has never been the will of God that faith should be easy (David M. McIntyre, Love's Keen Flame).

Please read Jeremiah 20.

Some years ago the *Queen Elizabeth 2*, Britain's biggest ocean liner at the time, underwent a complete refit. At a cost of millions of pounds this floating temple to self-indulgence was made more sumptuous than ever—at least, that was the plan. Contractors were working to a ridiculously tight deadline and were still engaged in some pretty major work as that deadline arrived and the passengers began to board. Holiday videos, shot by these passengers over the first few days, reveal just how far short the contractors had come to fulfilling their obligations. With half of the ship still resembling a building site, what had been sold as the cruise of a lifetime turned into a holiday nightmare, and it had to be abandoned just a few days into the trip, with passengers both refunded and compensated for their disappointment.

Disappointment can be measured in proportion to the strength of the expectation that went before it, and frequently the amount that we pay determines just what we expect. If the passengers had paid £30 a night for bed and breakfast they might have greeted the building works with a cheery grin and typically British remarks about making the best of a bad job. But because they had each forked out enough to keep the average family fed and clothed for a year, their expectations were correspondingly much higher and their disappointment was all the greater (although not as great as those who paid a similar fortune to sail on the *Titanic*). In this case, the tens of thousands of pounds they had parted with had been supposed to give several weeks of opulent and extravagant luxury, when in fact what they got was little better than a few nights in a cheap seaside hotel.

But, of course, money is not the only issue. Whenever people have high expectations that are not met, intense disappointment is the outcome— and the more important the organization, the bigger the disappointment when it fails. This explains the anger that arises when a government that has come to power promising wide-sweeping reforms fails to deliver. Or when a church allows child-abusing priests to continue their ministry. Or when God appears to let us down.

Disappointment with God?

I once remarked to a Christian friend that I was enjoying reading Philip Yancey's book *Disappointment with God*, but he surprised me by expressing his disapproval of the title. While accepting that people could be disappointed with the church, because it contained fallible men and women, he thought disappointment with God seemed almost too blasphemous to talk about. He pictured a self-important little man complaining about the way God had let him down (i.e. not given him what he wanted) and felt that it lent credibility to our sinful rebellion against God. Since God is perfect and cannot be blamed for sin, how could a book allow that people might be right to be disappointed with him? And yet disappointment with God is precisely what people do feel when everything goes wrong.

And the more important the organization, the bigger the disappointment when it fails.

It is interesting that in Jeremiah 20 God does not attempt to answer Jeremiah's complaint or tell him to stop whining. He allows the outcry to stand and does not censure Jeremiah for rudeness or a lack of faith, yet Christians usually feel threatened by such talk. If we start complaining to God about how he has let us down, where will it all end? Not everyone can bear the burden of listening to someone else's doubts, but if we do not allow Christians to express them, we end up stifling faith rather than nurturing it.

There are circles where the Christian life is presented in terms of undiluted victory and the confident expectation of continual success. There is such a thing as victory in the Christian life (look at Romans 8, for instance, which we will return to later in this book), but the type of faith that speaks only of triumph presents a completely skewed view of life, giving the impression that everything should always work out to our satisfaction.

What makes this sort of belief so serious is that in the end it undermines faith altogether. It promises the sort of life that most people wish they could attain, but when it cannot deliver on those promises it then gags the struggling believer. Speaking of failure and disappointment would not be acceptable in these circles, as it would mean questioning God and doubting him, so people are forced to either put up or shut up. Consequently some end up drifting away from the faith, feeling they have failed God badly, and perhaps also bitterly resenting the church for its failure to get to grips with reality. It is evident that groups like these have not encountered anyone like Jeremiah (perhaps they haven't even read his book!), or they would modify the way they talk. Jeremiah discovered that disappointment with God is real and that it is a profound test of faith. He also reveals that if it is faced and brought out into the open, under God's gaze, it can be resolved.

> God does not attempt to answer Jeremiah's complaint or tell him to stop whining.

One arm behind his back?

What makes Jeremiah's words of such value to us is that he is so deeply committed to God, to his truth, to the relevance of his message to the world, and to his people. He is not one of those perennial moaners who will always find something to complain about (and usually do it from the sidelines). Although Jeremiah complains on more than one occasion to God—and we get the word 'jeremiad', meaning a doleful complaint or lamentation, from his moaning—he is nevertheless not one of these carping individuals, so we need to sit up and take note of what he is saying.

The essence of his complaint is that, having been railroaded by God into his role as a prophet, he now feels that God has let him down. The immediate cause of this feeling is that he has endured a night in the stocks for a rather bold piece of prophetic symbolism that he had enacted the day before in full view of the city's leaders. At the beginning of chapter 18 Jeremiah had been instructed to go to a potter's house where he was given a message about Israel being an awkward lump of clay in God's hands, for him to mould as he pleased. This he then applied to the coming exile that would uproot the nation and send the Jews to Babylon. With this in mind, Jeremiah bought a pot, went out to one of the city gates where the leaders were assembled and smashed it in front of them to symbolize the message he was preaching—that irreparable disaster was coming on the city because it continued to rebel against God. Quite what he had expected from this dramatic gesture is not certain, but it is evident that he got more than he had bargained for. He had faced threats and plots before—there is evidence of a plot against him in chapter 11, in which the people of his home town of Anathoth, evidently embarrassed that one of their own number was such a thorn in the authorities' side, had threatened him with death if he did not stop prophesying—but on this occasion Jeremiah was actually attacked. Pashhur, a high official in the temple hierarchy—something like the head of security at the seat of a national government—had him arrested, beaten and placed in the stocks. These stocks were designed to hold the victim in an awkward, uncomfortable position (the original root of the word for this implement means to twist) that would have left him exhausted by the time he was released, so it is not to be wondered at that Jeremiah is feeling low by the time of his outburst. He did have something to say to Pashhur on his release—predicting once more the capture of the city by the Babylonians and the exile of the population, Pashhur among them—indicating that he was not completely cowed by the experience and had not forgotten his prophetic vocation. But it appears that giving the message again felt to Jeremiah like just so much bluster and bravado and that, in his spirit, he was completely crushed.

> Jeremiah discovered that disappointment with God is real and that it is a profound test of faith.

The principal element in his bitter complaint in verses 7–18 is that this is all God's fault. 'You deceived me … you overpowered me and prevailed' (v. 7). It is evident from Jeremiah's own words at the beginning of the book that he was rather reluctant to accept the mantle of a prophet, surprised at being called and very aware of his own unsuitability for the work. His primary reason for not wanting to accept the call from God was his youthfulness (look at 1:6), although quite how young he was is something we do not know. 2 Chronicles 34 tells us that Josiah, who was king when Jeremiah started his prophetic ministry, was just twenty when he began his purge of idol worship in Judea, so Jeremiah may have been similarly green. In an age when young people had no real voice in society, anyone under thirty would probably have found it difficult to be taken seriously, so Jeremiah's initial reaction is perfectly understandable. But he appears to have had no say in the matter. He was simply propelled into the task by God's call, and while he was given the reassurance that God would be with him and help him, it is evident that from his current vantage point this is not the sort of comfort he wants. His resentment against God's redirecting of his life into a ministry that constantly puts him in the firing line boils over in his prayers, and I must admit to some sympathy with him.

What choice did he have? The other well-known story of a reluctant prophet saw a man run from God and take a ship bound for the other end of the Mediterranean in an attempt to escape the call of God. Jeremiah would have known about Jonah unsuccessfully going AWOL, so it is possible that at one level he had just resigned himself to the inevitable: he couldn't win so he did as he was told. That would explain why he now explodes at God when the price of doing a job that he hadn't sought and delivering an unpopular message becomes unbearable. We should not think that this anger is a hatred of God. Rather, it is a passionately felt and plainly spoken complaint that his faithfulness to this calling as a prophet has brought him misery in two ways in particular, and that God has not stopped this from happening.

The unexpected cost of ministry

I know all the jokes about how easy it is to be a minister (only working one day a week, and all that), but as with any stereotype they do not deal with what it is really all about. The minister in the TV cartoon series *The*

Simpsons seems to capture what most people imagine to be the minister's personality and role: the Rev. Timothy Lovejoy is a rather insipid character who does little in life other than preach mildly boring sermons (to a full church, too!), hope that zealot Ned Flanders doesn't get too keen, and play with his train set. There is probably a whole bunch of reasons people might give for portraying ministers this way, but one is almost certainly that they have never understood what the real work of preaching and teaching the gospel actually entails. They probably imagine that the work is little more than a hobby, that it places no demands on either those who speak or those who listen, and they never dream that there might be some cost attached to doing it. After all, their congregations are attending voluntarily in their spare time, so what can there possibly be that might cause any stress?

The first area in which the cost appears concerns the nature of the message we are given and the way people respond to it. Jeremiah's message was not one of quiet persuasion, reasoning with people to change their ways, but an unrelenting series of searing rebukes that warned of disaster and God's judgement if people did not turn back to God. Take his first public message, in chapter 2, as an example. This was no gentle introduction to life as a prophet, for it was a broadside against a nation that had forsaken God, in which he castigated both the priests and the prophets for their failure to lead people back to God. If he had been hoping to win friends in high places by his adherence to the truth, he had gone the wrong way about it! Or later on, in chapter 7, where he stood at the gate to the temple and accused worshippers of hypocrisy, because they went on sinning against God yet assumed they were safe because they had the temple in their midst. His warning was brutally clear: God would remove the temple, just as he had taken away the sanctuary at Shiloh earlier in Israel's history, and the protection they falsely imagined they had would be gone.

The cost of this type of ministry is evident when we reach chapter 20. It is not just the beating and the night in the stocks that have so affected him, although they had certainly tipped him over the edge. It is the constant malicious whispering against him that he cannot live with. 'Terror on every side' was one of his regular turns of phrase—he used it against Pashhur, for instance—that was being used against him. 'There goes old Terror on every Side! Can you believe what he said yesterday? What an idiot! Someone ought to shut him up.' Mockery of this nature is commonplace. We are told that the famous eighteenth-century English actor David Garrick could impersonate preacher George Whitefield, whom he derisively called 'Dr Squintum', capturing his looks (including the squint), tone of voice and preaching style. Jeremiah was a similarly easy target. If he had been around today, British readers would be familiar with his catchphrases featuring on the TV quiz show *Have I got news for you,* and his mannerisms and voice patterns being used by Alistair McGowan to entertain the nation alongside impressions of David Beckham and Tony Blair.

This happens because, however carefully you phrase it, the good news is bad news first of all. Salvation is, by definition, salvation from something, and much as we would like to emphasise the benefits of being saved and talk about the gospel's joy, peace and reconciling power, we cannot do so unless people are actually saved. The power to forgive others is only available to those who have themselves seen their own need of forgiveness and that they need it as much as the murderer, rapist or child molester. When Peter and John were hauled before the Jewish ruling council in Acts 4 to account for their actions in healing a cripple, Peter left them in no doubt that the healing came through the power of Jesus Christ, but then also went on to spell out that salvation was only possible through the name of Jesus. On this occasion they received only threats, but in the next chapter the council was angry enough with the apostles' continued refusal to stop preaching about Jesus to come close to executing them. If the New Testament church had gone around healing people in the name of Jesus, but not saying that God wanted them to repent and put their faith in Jesus, it is quite likely the Jewish authorities would have left them alone. But you cannot separate those two aspects of the Christian faith and take the blessings without the belief, so there will always be pressure from those who do not like this aspect of the gospel for the church to tone down what it says and the way it says it. On occasions Christians succumb to that pressure.

In Galatians Paul rounds on members of a group, probably converted Pharisees like himself, who were trying to avoid paying this price by maintaining that Gentiles (that is, non-Jews) had to be circumcised in order to be true Christians. To do so, he says in 5:11, removes the offence of the cross. In order to be saved, sinful men and women, whether Jews or Gentiles, must put their trust in a crucified man who died under God's curse, rather than trust their own good deeds and religious living to make them acceptable to God. This was supremely offensive to both Jew and Gentile. Paul paid a high price for teaching it, in terms of being stoned at the hands of his own people, arrested and beaten. His caustic comment in 6:12 is that those who wanted to circumcise Gentiles were doing so out of fear of offending the Jews and suffering persecution as a result. What is surprising here is that this sort of opposition to the gospel was coming from within the church, just as Jeremiah's biggest problem came from religious people who professed faith in God. Faith must often be practised under pressure from those who ought to be on the same side, but they are not the only ones to create it.

What is dubbed 'political correctness' in Western society is just the latest version of a sinful world's attempts to blunt the edge of the Christian message and reduce it to something that is palatable and acceptable to everyone. This is certainly not to deny that it has anything to say to the church, for instance about racism, inequalities and accepting people, but the effect of many of its taboos is to tame God and push him into a corner where he cannot cause trouble by stopping people from having fun the way they want to. In such a society, people won't thank you for speaking out and will do everything they can to shut you up. Naturally, they will say that they respect your right to hold such opinions (whether they really do respect your right is a moot point if you look at the sort of legislation that is being debated by many Western governments), but you must keep them to yourself. I suspect that we are going to have to learn increasingly from Jeremiah on this subject because, like him, we have something to say that our society doesn't want to hear. Of course, there are ways of saying things and we shouldn't go out of our way to be deliberately offensive (it is possible to be persecuted for being a pain in the neck). But, accepting those caveats, we still have a message that is an offence to natural pride and we live in a society that is trying to squeeze God and his Word out altogether. So if we are going to be true to the God who gave his Word to us and the generations of believers who have suffered for their faithfulness to it, then, like Peter and his friends, there is no way that we can remain silent.

This leads us to the second of the unexpected costs of ministry: the effect of the message on those who preach it. The pressure of preaching a uniformly judgemental and permanently unpopular message was exacting a huge toll on Jeremiah, but he found that he could not just stop. That would be the easy option for someone who cared nothing for God, but Jeremiah could not entertain such a notion. The message, he says, is 'a fire shut up in my bones' (20:9) so that he could not hold it in even if he wanted to. It is here that his opening cry to God of being overpowered becomes clear. In understanding God's message to the nation he has also begun to feel something of God's anguish for the nation, his anger towards his own people who have turned to worship other gods and his grief over men and women who are heading for self-inflicted destruction. Try as he might, Jeremiah cannot escape this identification with God that now forces him towards public humiliation and rejection.

It is Jesus who warned his disciples that if the master suffered, so would the servants; but the New Testament writers never took this as a cause for defeatism, rather the reverse. Peter says in 1 Peter 4:13 that you should 'rejoice that you participate in the sufferings of Christ' because you are identifying so closely with him. When the apostle Paul says in 2 Corinthians 1:5 that the sufferings of Christ overflow into the lives of the Corinthian Christians, he also points out that the comfort of Christ comes with it so that they can pass it on to others. In Philippians 3:10 his prayer is that he might 'know Christ and the power of his resurrection and the fellowship of sharing in his sufferings'. Evangelicals in the West tend to omit the third part of that phrase when they quote it, because it doesn't fit with their experience. They want the power, but do not see that there is a price to pay.

I remember from Bible college that we students had a rather glamorous, even romantic, view of this notion of being compelled by God to preach. We pictured the God-driven eighteenth-century greats standing boldly before vast crowds, unflinchingly facing down the rabble and winning their hearts by the sheer passion of their oratory. Jeremiah, however, didn't feature in our model of a preacher. We only measured the cost of preaching faithfully in terms of whether someone might heave a brick in our direction or write a nasty letter to the press. It never occurred to me, at least, that identifying with God and his message might break the human spirit altogether.

Paul speaks of his own feelings in 2 Corinthians 11:28–29: 'Besides everything else, I face daily the pressure of my concern for all the churches. Who is weak, and I do not feel weak? Who is led into sin, and I do not inwardly burn?' If that seems rather tame, then turn to Galatians 4:19, where Paul expresses his passionate concern for a church that is being led astray and the intensity of his struggle for them that they might be restored to God: 'My dear children, for whom I am again in the pains of childbirth until Christ is formed in you …' After being present at the birth of my own children I came to realize what a staggering metaphor this is for pastoral work, why Christian growth can be so difficult, and why any involvement in pastoral care and leadership is at times one of the most frustrating and painful jobs around.

When I finished Bible college and was appointed to a church in the south-west of England our pastor's wife gave me and my wife a memorable send-off as we moved from Yorkshire to take up the post. She hugged us, smiled caringly and said simply, 'You're mad.' There wasn't a trace of bitterness in the way she said it, nor was it an attempt to stop us from going, it was just a down-to-earth Yorkshirewoman calling a spade a spade. She knew from experience what the real cost of ministry was and what we were letting ourselves in for. Looking back, I realize that I most certainly didn't.

By chapter 20 Jeremiah has paid this cost several times over and the inner conflict that is almost killing him as a result is evident as he prays. Although he had been warned at the very beginning that life as a prophet would get tough, perhaps he had not realized it would be this tough. More than likely, even though he was told about it, he simply did not understand the emotional cost of giving everything in delivering God's words and then being rejected, so the twelve verses of his prayer lurch violently from anger with God, through robust faith in God's power to deal with his persecutors, before they settle on a note of despair at the end.

This last feature of his prayer—almost a death wish—is most revealing, in that it not only indicates just how severe the opposition was, but also gives us hints about Jeremiah's personality. It is in the nature of introspective people to respond to conflict by internalizing their feelings, even taking it out on themselves, rather than attacking others. Depression, it is said, is anger turned in on yourself, so I think that what we are witnessing here is a quiet man who has not courted the limelight, struggling to deal with very personal attacks. Although he is praying to God about his situation, Jeremiah is nevertheless turning his intense anger and disappointment with God, as well as his feelings for those who had persecuted him, back in on himself in the form of wishing he had never been born. Children who are bullied may contemplate suicide. Victims of abuse may harm themselves and self-destruct. Jeremiah simply wants to be blotted out.

This is not the way it should be!

I can hear Jeremiah's disbelief about his circumstances, because I have felt it myself. 'This shouldn't happen—not to anyone, and especially not to me! People—believing men and women—shouldn't behave like that. How can they say such things?' The disappointment is all the greater because we know that God could put things right, by sweeping away opposition or changing the hearts and minds of those who cause us such grief, but instead he leaves us to deal with them. Basically we feel that these things shouldn't happen because God shouldn't allow them to happen, and yet he does. In fact, more than God merely letting these things happen, he seems to specialize in putting us in circumstances that test our expectations of him, in which he simply doesn't do what we think he should (or, conversely, does what we think he shouldn't). This is a recurring dilemma for believers: even though we may act in obedience to God's commands and with his help, events often go in completely the opposite direction to the one we had expected. It is almost as if he builds up our hopes and then seems to dash them to the ground.

Disappointment is all the greater because we know that God could put things right.

When Moses was appointed to lead Israel out of captivity in Egypt, he faced early disappointment when Pharaoh not only refused to let Israel go—that much he had been warned of—but also made their conditions worse. Ordering his foremen to treat the Israelites even more harshly and force them to collect their own straw to make the same quota of bricks as before, Pharaoh hoped to squash any thought of freedom quickly (Exodus 5). And, looking at the Israelite reaction, you can see that he might have succeeded. Turning on Moses and Aaron they blamed them for getting their hopes up and promising freedom, when all they had achieved was to make life worse. If God was in this plan, then surely he would keep the Israelites on Moses' side? It shouldn't happen this way!

When John Paton landed in 1858 on the South Sea island of Tanna in the New Hebrides (now called Vanuatu), he expected difficulties. Previous visits from missionaries had been greeted with spears, and one couple had been killed within minutes of landing. Difficult it certainly was, although not initially in the way he had foreseen. In under a year both his young wife (she was not twenty years old) and their first baby were dead, killed not by the cannibals who inhabited the island, but by a fever that carried off scores of Western missionaries soon after their arrival in tropical climes. If God was going to transform cannibals into Christians, why did he go so close to ending the project in its infancy? It shouldn't happen this way!

It shouldn't happen this way? Shouldn't it? The apostle Paul tells us in 2 Corinthians 1 that the threats he faced in the province of Asia (perhaps in Ephesus) were so serious that they were under 'great pressure, far beyond our ability to endure, so that we despaired even of life. Indeed, in our hearts we felt the sentence of death …' (1:8–9). He then goes on to explain that 'this happened that we might not rely on ourselves but on God, who raises the dead', and in so doing he gives us the key to understanding why in fact it must happen this way.

The curse of self-reliance

It would be a mistake to think that, just because we live in a culture that exalts human achievements and the ability to get the job done, we have the monopoly on self-confidence. It is a universal feature of human nature to believe that, in the spiritual realm, we have got what it takes. This primarily takes the form of a self-righteousness that believes I possess sufficient goodness to make myself acceptable to God. The gospel knocks that one squarely on the head and insists that none of us is righteous by nature, nor can we earn God's favour by adding good, or even religious, deeds to our spiritual CV. The only answer lies in trusting completely in Jesus Christ, accepting him as the Saviour who not only covers our sins (which includes everything we had previously thought was good) before God, but who clothes us with his perfection so that we are acceptable in God's sight. To paraphrase a hymn, when God looks in my direction, he sees Jesus and forgives me.[1] Self-reliance has no place before God.

Christians may accept this and yet fall foul of self-confidence in another guise, in the form of a belief that, since God calls them his co-workers, it is their abilities and strengths that will see the task through. In twenty-first century Western churches this self-confidence is most likely to break through in the areas of management techniques and the pursuit of excellence. I have no basic objection to these two things. The insights of management techniques are very helpful in understanding the process of growth, analysing the church's leadership structures or framing a vision, for instance. And excellence in public ministry is a good aim, because so many of the people we are trying to reach are used to the high-power presentations of the media and will look down disdainfully on (or may not even look at) our sometimes rather shoddy attempts at communication. Where the danger lies for us is in assuming that because we have formulated a six-point vision, have full-colour brochures, slick marketing and presentation, a professional worship band and our songs projected from a computer, we are then going to be more successful. But that is the classic mistake. I'll always remember the cartoons in Michael Green's book *Evangelism—Now and Then*. The front cover pictures two preachers in action. One man, evidently from the first century (he is wearing the typical Christmas story dressing gown), is in full flow, equipped with nothing more than a scroll and a big smile. The other is a speaker from the twentieth century (the book came out in 1979), complete with tape player, PA system and instructions on how to evangelise, but for all this technological back-up (and we would add even more to that today), he looks unsure of himself. The final chapter of the book backs this up further. It is prefaced with a cartoon of a huge lorry, piled high with yet more audio-visual equipment, driven by a rather nervous man who is thinking to himself, 'I'm sure I've forgotten something …' Significantly, the chapter that follows is about the power of the Spirit in evangelism.

The temptation to trust techno-wizardry rather than the life-giving Spirit is the same now as it was in 1979. In fact that danger has always been around in one form or another, and just because Paul didn't have access to a mobile phone or e-mail did not mean that the temptation to trust human abilities rather than God was any the weaker. From his letters to the Corinthian church we gather that one of the temptations he faced was to use a more impressive, discursive style of oratory that would have appealed to the Greek mind. There is little doubt that Paul could have spoken this way—he had both the intellect and the training to do it—but he tells us in 1 Corinthians 2:1,4–5 that he chose a different way: 'I did not come with eloquence or superior wisdom' and 'my message and my preaching were not with wise and persuasive words, but with a demonstration of the Spirit's power, so that your faith might not rest on men's wisdom, but on God's power.' Using his more normal, simple style of explaining about Jesus, he chose a method that meant he had to rely on the Spirit's power to convince his hearers, rather than a method that would have impressed them with him. If he had done that and perhaps wowed his audience with his brilliance, they would then have come to trust in the wisdom (brilliance, charisma, personality, etc.) of the speaker, rather than in God.

The strength of weakness

It is for this reason that what Jeremiah faced, and the hardships Paul described in 2 Corinthians 1, are the way things will be: so that we might not rely on ourselves. This is not to say that every scheme or plan we make will collapse around our ears, nor must everything we do end in disaster if it is to see God's blessing on it. But it is only when we are at the end of our own resources that we discover the richest extent of God's power, so the greatest need we have is to rely on him rather than ourselves.

> It is for this reason that what Jeremiah faced, and the hardships Paul described in 2 Corinthians 1, are the way things will be: so that we might not rely on ourselves.

The natural response to such talk is to fear that if we accept this notion we will lose out in some way. Everything in us tells us we will not be as successful if we are not in control, if we don't have the biggest and best, or if we are weak. But God tells us the opposite and puts us in situations that prove his point. Paul made this painful (literally) discovery and tells us about it in 2 Corinthians 12, in the clearest statement of this principle that we have. He tells us that he was privileged to see visions of God that were so awesome that he simply could not say exactly what happened. He says he was transported to heaven, so it was probably something along the lines of John's visions in Revelation, but he was not entirely sure, so we can't be either. What happened then, he says, is that 'to keep me from becoming conceited because of these surpassingly great revelations, there was given me a thorn in my flesh, a messenger of Satan, to torment me' (12:7). Once again, he does not define what this thorn was, but it was evidently something that caused him enough distress to pray several times that God would remove it. Yet God refused his requests with the significant words, 'My grace is sufficient for you, for my power is made perfect in weakness' (12:9).

If there is anything that cuts across the success-driven, self-confident, wrinkle-free generation that we live in (and that the church sometimes tries to emulate), this is it. I once saw a video of an evangelistic presentation by a team of bodybuilders who could break baseball bats in their hands, tear up telephone directories and pick up several members of the audience at the same time. Their message was that those who followed Jesus weren't wimps, which I guess is true, but I could not help wondering firstly whether the Bible's talk of a suffering Saviour wasn't getting lost in what they were doing, and secondly whether they were not going too far in their desire to avoid being labelled 'wimps'. The meeting was like a contest to find the strongest man in the world as they pumped iron and strained to perform increasingly impressive feats of strength. I couldn't doubt their sincerity or faith, but the image that came across was of their own muscles honed to perfection, chiselled features and youthful energy that could take heaven by storm, rather than weak people trusting in the strength of a mighty God.

The trouble with such clean-cut health and dynamism is that it can suggest that you have to be a winner to follow Jesus and, in the words of one of rock band Queen's most stirring anthems, that God has no time for losers. That song—'We are the Champions'—is played across the world at sporting finals, because of its obvious relevance to the victors in a contest.

Yet it is also an ironically apt description of our society's attitude towards the rest, those who don't emerge victorious, or the people at the bottom of the pile. Everybody worships the celebrities but has no time for losers, so it would be tragic if the church gave the impression that these were its priorities, too.

This is why God's greats tend to be wounded and, rather like the patriarch Jacob in Genesis, walk with a limp because they have met with God and follow a crucified leader. Their weakness will keep them in touch with the broken people they live with, at the same time as ensuring that it is God's power that operates through them. And the phrase 'my power is made perfect in weakness' means that they don't lose out at all. Rather they gain and achieve more than they would have done if they had been strong. If this is hard to believe, it is because it doesn't look like this when you emerge, stiff and cold, from a night in the stocks, when the authorities despise you as a thorn in their side, when your name is a byword among the locals and the only people who seem to listen to you are enemies looking for something to use against you. But believe it you must.

> Their weakness will keep them in touch with the broken people they live with, at the same time as ensuring that it is God's power that operates through them.

In 1866 Welsh missionary Robert J. Thomas joined an American expedition up the Taedong River that was attempting to make contact with the city of Pyongyang in Korea. This nation had been closed to all outside influence until then, so the purpose of the trip was primarily commercial, but Thomas managed to persuade the sponsors to give him and a crate of Christian literature space on board *The General Sherman*. As the vessel moved upstream he was able to give out tracts and copies of the Scriptures to those he met, and leave copies on the river bank when people fled from the foreigners who landed. At Pyongyang, however, they encountered a hostile reaction that prevented landing and eventually decided to leave without establishing relations with the citizens, but the ship ran aground as it navigated some rapids and became stuck fast. The locals seized their chance to attack with fire boats, so the crew were forced to abandon the burning ship and wade for shore, where all were quickly killed. One man's conduct stood out. While the crew fought to the last, Thomas came ashore with an armful of books which he threw into the crowd of his attackers and attempted to give to those who clubbed him down. A more futile gesture you could hardly imagine, unless you believe that God's power is made perfect in weakness. Twenty-seven years later, when the nation was open to outside contact and churches were being planted, missionary leaders catechized the son of one of the men who had received one of these Bibles from Robert Thomas. More significantly than just one or two copies of the Bible appearing was the dramatic growth of the church in Korea. From complete resistance to the gospel in the mid-nineteenth century to revival in the early twentieth and sustained growth, South Korea has emerged in the twenty-first century as one of the primary missionary sending nations of the world. Human weakness paved the way for God's power.[2]

As this incident demonstrates, this hidden power is not some potion or magic formula that suddenly transforms us into superheroes, so that we lose all our fears, become invulnerable and save the day. Comic book hero Asterix and his Gallic companions may be able to do things this way with the help of the druid Getafix and his brew, but they remain on the pages of a book. The real strength that lies in our weakness is not only not ours, it is in fact quite likely that we will not even realize it is operating. John Stott relates how he spoke at a convention one year when he was just recovering from a bout of flu that had left him weak in body and voice. He could hardly deliver his message, but struggled through and sat down, exhausted and rather dejected, feeling that it had been a waste of time for the congregation. Yet over the years he had more people comment about how greatly they had been helped by that message than for any of his other sermons. In his weakness he discovered God's strength. It didn't stop him feeling weak, but it was there nevertheless.

And because it was there, God brought unexpected results that would not have been seen if it had been his own speaking skills that he depended

> The real strength that lies in our weakness is not only not ours, it is in fact quite likely that we will not even realize it is operating.

on. As Paul says in 2 Corinthians 1:9, the God we are called to rely on raises the dead. There is no situation so desperate that God cannot bring out of it something that glorifies him, that works to change what looks beyond redemption, and that even works for our good. After a night in the stocks Jeremiah found this hard to believe and told God as much, but God's power was still at work through his words. Jeremiah was the one who was right about the fate of the city, not the scores of spin-doctor prophets who said everything would soon return to normal. He was one of the few who were treated leniently by the Babylonians when they entered the city, because he had risked being thought a traitor for recommending surrender. And it was Jeremiah who spoke accurately about the length of the exile in Babylon and that the nation would return to its land in the future. It is just that, from the twisted perspective of the stocks, he could not see that he was right. The pain of the treatment he received and the bitter sting of disappointment temporarily blinded him to the real situation: God was speaking to the nation through him.

> The pain of the treatment he received and the bitter sting of disappointment temporarily blinded him to the real situation: God was speaking to the nation through him.

I have heard it said that you won't realize that God is all you need until he is all you've got. If God has placed you in a situation where your weakness and inadequacy are exposed, try to see that, at some point or other, it must happen this way. Only then are you likely to appreciate that his grace is enough for you and that his power is more truly revealed through your weakness than it would be through your strength. Once you have grasped that, while disappointments will still come, you will find it possible to look at them in a different way. Not with a cheery grin so much as a firm confidence that God is at work, and a deep contentedness that his strength will more than make up for your weakness.

Summary: Disappointment is necessary to bring us to rely on God.

Key verse: 2 Corinthians 12:9: 'My grace is sufficient for you, for my power is made perfect in weakness.'

To think about: Have there been times in my life when I have been intensely disappointed with God? How does it help me to realize that my weakness and failure pave the way for God's power?

'How long must I wrestle with my thoughts and every day have sorrow in my heart?', Psalm 13:2.

'My tears have been my food day and night, while men say to me all day long, "Where is your God?"' Psalm 42:3.

'Why are you downcast, O my soul? Why so disturbed within me? Put your hope in God, for I will yet praise him, my Saviour and my God', Psalm 42:5.

Thinking more deeply

The degree of our peace is tied to our prayer life … This is not because prayer is psychologically soothing, but because we address a prayer-answering God, a personal God, a responding God, a sovereign God whom we can trust with the outcomes of life's confusions. And we learn, with time, that if God in this or that instance does not choose to take away the suffering, or utterly remove the evil, *he does send grace and power.*

Don Carson on Philippians 4:6–7, *How long, O Lord?*

Notes

1 **Charitie Lees De Chenez,** 'Before the throne of God above'.
2 This story of Robert Thomas is taken from **William Blair and Bruce Hunt,** *The Korean Pentecost* (Edinburgh: The Banner of Truth Trust, 1977), pp. 26–31.

My story

Betrayed

To protect the identity of the writer and her family, this account has been written anonymously.

One morning, on what I expected to be a normal, happy day, my world crumbled when I discovered that my husband had been having an affair. The feeling of suffocation and nightmare lasted for a very long time, as I fought to make sense of what my faith in the Lord Jesus meant in a time of such betrayal and hurt.

At the beginning of this whole trauma I quickly told my husband that I forgave him—that was a lie. It was what I wished was the truth, but it was not—I wasn't ready or able to know what those words meant. Having been brought up in a Christian home, with such lovely examples in my parents of love and forgiveness, I knew that this was something I should do—but how? Not just words and pushing the hurt down to erupt later, but genuine on-the-cross stuff. That was my big problem. Struggling to stay afloat in a drowning situation is about the best description of my feelings. Emotions raged and almost swept me away. Reason, academic arguments about the fallenness of human nature, the necessity for understanding—all these were a long distance away. I was extremely angry towards both my husband and God. I felt that my Lord and Saviour had let me down, had let my husband slip out of his hands, and that my heavenly Father had either forgotten me, or was punishing me for not being a better person. I even felt that the death of my husband would at least have been a normal trauma and not a betrayal. Extreme bitterness and feeling justified in blaming and raging kept me going.

Fear also gripped me whenever I was alone—fear of nothing ever being stable again and of never being able to trust anyone; fear that our marriage would not survive; that the children would come to hate me or my husband if they ever found out; that people in general would think that this was something bound to happen to me because I wasn't good enough. Worst of all was the fear that the Rock—my God—was a crumbling rock after all.

But, gradually, verses I knew well kept rearing their heads: 'Bear with each other and forgive *whatever* grievances you may have against one another. Forgive as the Lord forgave you' (Colossians 3:13). 'Forgive us our debts, *as we also have forgiven our debtors*' (Matthew 6:12). Such Scriptures enraged me at first—so demanding and so hard. Why does he ask such impossible things of us? Of me?

And then there was the rediscovery of the Psalms. All my emotions, questions and doubts, the psalmist had experienced. 'Even my close friend, whom I trusted, he who shared my bread, has lifted up his heel against me' (Psalm 41:9). 'If an enemy were insulting me I could endure it; if a foe were raising himself against me, I could hide from him. But it is you, a man like myself, my companion, my close friend, with whom I once enjoyed sweet fellowship as we walked with the throng at the house of God' (Psalm 55:12–14). 'I am confined and cannot escape; my eyes are dim with grief … Why, O LORD, do you reject me and hide your face from me?' (Psalm 88:8–9,14). I found that not only did the psalmist understand, but he was able to come out at the other end of trouble with praise on his lips. Could I do that too?

At first I just wallowed in the release of seeing my feelings written by God's people thousands of years ago and skipped over the fact that change needed to occur within me so that I could come back into the light. In some ways, staying in misery and grief and refusing to forgive is the easier option because no effort is needed—it just comes naturally. But once the decision is taken to do as the Lord wants, effort has to be made. So a new phase of pilgrimage had to start.

Slowly, so slowly that it was almost imperceptible, the fact of the Lord's faithfulness and love became real again. He hadn't abandoned me, but I had been too numb to feel that love surrounding me. He still 'stood within the shadow, keeping watch above his own'.[1] The words of Scripture from Isaiah became real: 'Fear not, for I have redeemed you; I have called you by name; you are mine. When you pass through the waters, I will be with you; and when you pass through the rivers, they will not sweep over you. When you walk through the fire, you will not be burned [you may be scorched, though!]; the flames will not set you ablaze' (Isaiah 43:1–2). Time and again verses declaring and affirming that God *is* a sure rock forced themselves on my mind. 'My soul finds rest in God alone; my salvation comes from him. He alone is my rock and my salvation; he is my fortress, I shall never be shaken' (Psalm 62:1–2). Words like these soothed fear away and were like an antibiotic treating my disease of un-love both of self and others.

The reconstruction work, as I now see it, had its foundations laid. If these Scriptures meant so much to me in terms of comfort and the knowledge of God's love then I had to respond by doing the things he asked of me. Very falteringly I began to think that one day I might actually 'get rid of all bitterness, rage and anger' and 'forgive, just as in Christ God forgave [me]' (Ephesians 4:31–32). The decision had to be made to take these commands on board and try to obey rather than wallow in grief and bitterness for life. I had by now, of course, realized that my maturity as a Christian had not been what I had imagined. I was learning the hard way how stubborn my heart was; how, without my Lord Jesus I was as nothing; that my pride and refusal to forgive were every bit as sinful as adultery and murder. Maybe they didn't hurt other people quite as much, but they hurt my heavenly Father. The evening when both of us, weeping, acknowledged our nothingness before the Lord was one of the high points of our marriage—we had each other in the right perspective and now know how very fallible we both are, so we could have a free and more fulfilling love for each other, making allowances for each other's shortcomings.

Here are some of the key lessons I have learnt:

- I have to follow my Lord to the cross and be willing for the pain of forgiveness. It is costly and at times almost unbearable. Once the decision to forgive was taken, it had to be treated as a vow, which I'm ashamed to say I broke many times, until one day I figuratively buried the whole episode and walked away.
- Holding on to the 'smaller' sins is counter-productive. They are insidious and grow roots and then shoots which ruin fellowship with the Lord and others—and consequently turn me into a bitter woman.
- Only the Lord is our Rock, always completely dependable, never letting us down—absolutely reliable.

- Our God does what he promises. The Comforter does come—as the root meaning of the word says—as the one who strengthens.
- I must examine my motives and the direction of my will: is it towards my heavenly Father?
- I have choices, all the time, to do as my Lord wishes, or not. There is such a short moment when the decision hangs in the balance; to pour out the bitter words and angry reproaches, or take a deep breath and ask the Holy Spirit to calm my thoughts.
- When I take him at his word I *do* experience his help. 'Before they call I will answer; while they are still speaking I will hear' (Isaiah 65:24).
- Our heavenly Father only allows in the lives of his children what he can use to make them more like Jesus. He can certainly bring good out of evil.

Note

1 From **James Russell Lowell,** 'Once to every man and nation'.

8 Prosperity:
The gecko in the kettle

Remembering God in the good times

Adversity hath slain her thousand; prosperity her ten thousand'
(Thomas Brooks, Precious Remedies against Satan's Devices).

Please read Deuteronomy 8.

Take a frog and toss it into a pan of boiling water and it will, not surprisingly, jump straight out. But put it in when the water is cold and then heat it slowly and it will not notice. Apparently it will stay in the water while the temperature rises, right until it boils and it is literally cooked alive. I have no intention of repeating this experiment to see how true it is (and while I have read about it on several occasions, I have not come across anyone who actually admits to having conducted it), but I do have a friend who has inadvertently seen it fulfilled with geckos. Working in the Seychelles for a couple of years, he and his wife became quite accustomed to these small, lizard-like creatures that were everywhere on the island. They would get into the house and find their way into anything without a tight-fitting lid, which was not normally a great problem as they were not dangerous, but on a few occasions their exploring took them to places that were dangerous for geckos and a number came to a grisly end as a result. One took up residence in a toaster, where it was roasted before anyone knew it was there, while another, as the chapter title suggests, found its way into the kettle. My friend said they did not notice anything, except that for several months cups of tea had a strange flavour. They put this down to the local water supply, until cleaning the kettle out one day revealed the shrivelled corpse of an unfortunate gecko.

Whether it happens to frogs or geckos, the point is that we may find ourselves in (or, more to the point, put ourselves in) an environment that is far more damaging than we realize, but because we live with it and have grown accustomed to it we do not see what it is doing to us. Living in a culture that has more spare cash than it knows what to do with, we are bombarded with messages telling us to enjoy life to the full and spend more on ourselves than is healthy, while charitable giving is usually reduced to scraping together any spare change we might have. As Christians we assume that we are not unduly affected by living in this atmosphere, when the Bible is far more realistic. It has more teaching about money than almost any other subject, and its warnings about the negative effects of the misuse of money should strike a chord with us in the prosperous West. Because we live in a society that is committed to outrageous excess we do not see what effect it has on faith, but the Bible leaves us in no doubt. We are in hot water, the steam is beginning to curl around our nostrils and we are slowly being boiled alive.

Falling from a great height

If we are not aware of the potential danger to faith from living in a prosperous environment it is because we do not take seriously enough the warnings and examples contained in the pages of Scripture. It is not that the Bible is anti-money. Rather, as the often misquoted 1 Timothy 6:10 points out, it is the *love* of money that is the root of all kinds of evil, not money itself, and we are fools if we think we are immune from that temptation. Yet perhaps more powerful than the warnings on this subject are the examples—and there are quite a few—of good men who succumbed to the negative effect of prosperity. Having started well when times were hard and they had to trust in God, they stumbled badly once life was easier and the pressure was off.

> We are in hot water, the steam is beginning to curl around our nostrils and we are slowly being boiled alive.

The accounts of the lives of Judah's kings in 2 Chronicles are particularly revealing in this regard. Asa, for example (2 Chronicles 14–16), is recorded as a king who did what was right in God's eyes. His long reign started with an active faith in God that led him to purge the nation once again of its foreign idols, and when a foreign army suddenly invaded he turned to God for help. His prayer before the battle is a model of dependence upon God, recognizing that the powerless find strength in God: 'Help us, O LORD our God, for we rely on you, and in your name we have come against this vast army' (14:11). When victory came Asa took courage to push the reforms of the nation further, even to the point of deposing his own grandmother from her position as queen mother because she worshipped the goddess Asherah, and to lead the people in making a covenant that they would seek God with all their heart and soul (15:12). The account records that 'they sought God eagerly, and he was found by them. So the LORD gave them rest on every side' (15:15).

But something changed after this. The account jumps to the end of Asa's reign, to the thirty-sixth year, after a period of peace, stability and prosperity, when Baasha the king of the northern kingdom of Israel suddenly threatened to invade. Asa's reaction this time was to go to the Arameans, traditionally some of the local troublemakers, and form an alliance with them against Israel to remove the threat. The ploy succeeded, but earned Asa a rebuke from one of the prophets: how could he not trust in God to help them (16:7–9)? It wasn't the cost of his actions that mattered (although he paid a fair sum) so much as the lack of faith in God. In the past God had delivered them from a vast army, so he could have done it again without the help of some of the region's more unpleasant characters. As Hanani the prophet pointed out, 'The eyes of the LORD range throughout the earth to strengthen those whose hearts are fully committed to him', so why couldn't Asa have faith that God would help them again?

We are not given an answer to that question, but what Asa did next gives us a fairly good indication of what was going on. Enraged by the prophet's rebuke, he threw the man into prison and clamped down on other dissenting voices. A few years later, the account tells us, he was 'afflicted with a disease in his feet. Though his disease was severe, even in his illness he did not seek help from the LORD, but only from the physicians' (16:12). It might be reading too much into the text to conclude that this disease was gout, a complaint most frequently of the rich, brought on by too much rich food, wine and a life of ease, but this is certainly what it looks like. Something like twenty-five years without stress, trouble or threat had induced laziness and indolence that now caught up with him. More significantly, those years had also generated a crippling spiritual lethargy that had completely sapped his faith in God, so that when a threat arose he had no spiritual resources to call on. His courage, which had previously stemmed from his trust in God, simply melted away. And then when God spoke to correct him he rejected it violently and shut himself off from God. The significance of the comment about only using his physicians is not that the Bible thinks doctors have nothing to offer. Rather, it is the last piece of a tragic picture that is being painted for us. From having a king with a vibrant faith at the beginning who sought God in everything, at the end we now have a bitter old man, a shadow of his former self, who no longer thinks God has anything to offer.

> Something like twenty-five years without stress, trouble or threat had induced laziness and indolence that now caught up with him. More significantly, those years had also generated a crippling spiritual lethargy that had completely sapped his faith in God.

If Asa were the only example of success and prosperity causing a miserable decline in faith, that on its own would be bad enough, but sadly he is not. Uzziah provides another sobering example in 2 Chronicles 26. Here is another king who started off under difficult circumstances—in this case he had to contend with the murder of his father and rebuild the nation—but he turned to God who made him successful in everything he did. The account lists his achievements in battle and a military rebuilding programme that significantly strengthened the walls of Jerusalem and reformed the army, while a brief mention of national prosperity has a hint of a party political broadcast about it as it talks of full employment. But the list ends with a revealing observation: 'His fame spread far and wide, for he was greatly helped until he became powerful. But after Uzziah became powerful, his pride led to his downfall' (26:15–16).

We are given no insight into his thought processes at this time other than that one deadly word: pride. In a moment of irrational stupidity, egged on by foolish pride and perhaps driven by annoyance that the temple was the one area where he did not give the orders, he entered the temple and started to burn incense at the altar, a task only performed by the priests and forbidden to anyone outside the tribe of Levi. When confronted by the high priest and told to stop, his reaction was similar to Asa's and he flew into a rage. Lesser men would have been executed on the spot for such blasphemy. Centuries before, two of Aaron's own sons had died before the Lord for offering what was called 'unauthorized fire' (Leviticus 10), but in this case leprosy broke out on Uzziah's head. Realizing that this was a judgement from God and that worse was to come if he didn't stop, was glad to make his exit then and escape with his life, but he spent the rest of his days in isolation and was probably rarely ever seen in public again.

In both these cases the prelude to a spectacular fall was an extended period of success and prosperity—and there are other examples along the same lines that could be cited. Both faced severe tests at the beginning of their reign that forced them into a corner where trust in God was the only option. Frightening as those circumstances were, faith was strongest when facing them and the success each achieved later came out of the faith exercised during that troubled period. Yet when peace came and the nation enjoyed a period of prosperity, faith in God waned, probably imperceptibly at first. Neither Asa nor Uzziah became atheists and civil life in Israel still revolved around the appointed religious festivals, but at some point the heart of it all died and it became a ritual that could be repeated without thinking, just something that was part of the calendar. And for the king it lost its personal significance, as the urgent need to trust God faded into the background. All that was needed then was a crisis to put pressure on this hollow excuse for faith and it collapsed.

> It seems quite logical to believe that faith can only blossom if growing conditions are favourable and that a harsh environment will stunt growth, but both Scripture and experience turn this logic on its head.

Upside-down thinking

The reason we are shocked by these examples of decline and fall is that we have lived for so long with the quite natural assumption that adversity harms faith, while prosperity benefits it. It seems quite logical to believe that faith can only blossom if growing conditions are favourable and that a harsh environment will stunt growth, but both Scripture and experience turn this logic on its head.

Church growth around the world continually demonstrates that faith not only survives under pressure, it often thrives. The observation by the second-century church leader Tertullian that 'the blood of the martyrs is the seed of the church' has been borne out in every century since he spoke those words, but the pressure does not need to be as extreme as that to prove the point. Across the world, the churches that are most vibrant are located in the developing nations, while churches in the rich and prosperous West tend to be moribund, lacking in spiritual fervour, or in what seems like terminal decline. This is not to say that prosperity is evil and should be shunned. Deuteronomy 8 is one of the places where the Bible unashamedly describes God's goodness in terms of a prosperous environment. Nor are adversity, poverty and hardship good things in themselves. It is simply that the effect in the spiritual realm of these two opposites is frequently the reverse of what most people expect. This contrast is, for instance, starkly visible when comparing the state of the church in Eastern and Western Europe.

During the years of Communist dictatorship in the second half of the twentieth century, the church in Eastern Europe was under considerable pressure from cynical atheistic authorities who did everything to undermine both the church and individual faith. In order to support Christians during these years couriers would visit beleaguered pastors, take Bibles, medication and basic necessities, and preach in house meetings, and all would return with stories of the heroic faith and courage of the Christians they encountered. Even as we in the West were praying for them that they would remain faithful to the Lord Jesus and not deny him when they lost their jobs or were thrown into prison, we recognized that their faith was more vital and real than ours. Tape recordings of their prayer meetings demonstrated a fervour that we could never imagine possessing—they were, after all, praying about life and death, while we tended to be thinking about whether the time had come to change the car or whether we could get a parking space in town. Their insatiable desire to read the Bible, which they did not have in large quantities, was mirrored by our own complacency with the many copies we had lying around the house. And their church meetings were full, packed to the doors in many cases with people of all ages eager to listen to long sermons, while ours were half empty or worse, with people who complained if the pastor went over half an hour and ensured that Sunday lunch was burned to a crisp. All in all, reports from these countries left me feeling that, even though we were doing something important in giving encouragement and providing basic necessities, we were the ones who needed prayer to remain faithful.

The Russian poet Irina Ratushinskaya has an interesting reflection on the deadening effect living in the West has on faith, compared to the revitalizing effect that living under Communism had on faith:

> A person who is deprived of everything, of family, of contact with friends, who is totally isolated, alone, without any property at all, not even a toothbrush, has nothing left to lose. An enormous, powerful sense of security follows. Instead of panic, one feels God's hand on one's shoulder. We all felt nothing really bad could happen to us: we all thought, 'If they kill us today, tomorrow we will be in heaven.'

When I came to the West, I thought, 'Now I'm in a world of holidaymakers.'

> I wish I had the same feeling now, but I don't. Under such pressure, God feels really close: it's easier to serve God when in trouble than on holiday. When I came to the West, I thought, 'Now I'm in a world of holidaymakers.'

> When Jesus came, he said, 'Leave everything you have.' That was a frightening demand. A person can only develop if he or she is able to let go. It was easier for us to take risks back in the Russian labour camps because we had nothing to lose. Now, after spending ten years in the West, I do have something to lose.[1]

That was probably the experience of Christians right across the Communist world. Even today, Eastern European churches tend to be bigger and faster growing than Western European equivalents. But with the demise of Communism the situation has changed, at least in some ways. While the hoped-for prosperity has not arrived, people are basically free, so it will be interesting to see how they cope with that over the next twenty years or so. Will they retain that vital faith, or will the pressure of living in a world of holidaymakers (or aspiring to live in that world) take its toll? If our experience is anything to go by, it is difficult to see how they can avoid being adversely affected.

Don't say you weren't warned

But it is not as if we have not been warned about this hazard. The danger is spelled out on numerous occasions, the clearest and most detailed of these being from the lips of Moses. In Deuteronomy Moses is addressing the tribes of Israel as they stand on the borders of Canaan, preparing to enter and take the land after forty years of living in the desert. Moses, however, knows he will not be accompanying them, because God has told him that he will die on this side of the Jordan, so his message consists of reminders of how God has helped them and exhortations to continue to trust him. Those forty years spent in the desert had not been part of the original plan, but came about because the people had lost courage first time around and refused to believe that God could defeat the opposition that awaited them. At Kadesh Barnea, on the southern edge of Canaan, they had rebelled against God, and had even talked of stoning Moses and returning to Egypt. This open rebellion cost them dearly, as God took their unbelief at face value: those who said that God could not get them in safely would not enter. A whole generation was therefore condemned to wander in the wilderness until they died out, after which their children would enter instead of them.

When we come in on his message in chapter 8, Moses is speaking about the lessons they should have learned from this difficult past and how they should apply it to the future. This chapter is cleverly organized in the way it is written and has a clear central point in verse 11: 'Be careful that you do not forget the LORD your God.' The subjects around this verse urge the Israelites both to remember that God helped them in the hard times they experienced in the past, and not forget God when life is much easier in Canaan. You should note that the same upside-down thinking we identified earlier is evident here, too: the wilderness, a place of judgement and hardship, was also a place where God blessed his people and provided for them; the land of Canaan, a place of rich blessing, could also become a snare and lead them away from God.

Chapter 8 verses 1–5 and 15–16 review the lessons of the nation's recent tragic past and it is at once apparent that Moses does not view these years as completely lost. God had remained with the nation all the time they were in the desert and Moses has a strong sense of God's purpose in everything that happened. His first aim was to 'humble' the Israelites (v. 2) after their rebellion—this word can mean to either punish or discipline someone, and no doubt both meanings are in view here, since the wilderness was both a punishment for those who disobeyed God and a means of disciplining and training those who experienced it. In fact, in 8:5 Moses summarizes the whole period spent in the desert as a time when God was disciplining them as a father would do with his children. Secondly, God's intention was to 'test you in order to know what was in your heart, whether or not you would keep his commands.' In other places (such as 6:16) Moses points out that the Israelites were testing God by their actions, refusing to believe that he would be true to his word and wanting him to prove that he could help them. But the other side of the coin is that God was testing them. He wanted to know whether they would continue to trust him and whether they were devoted to him at heart—that is, what their principal attitude would be to him in such events, whether it would be one of faith or unbelief. He knew what their parents' attitude was. He wanted to know what the children had learned from the experience. We can say that this is always God's concern: when hard times arrive, will you trust him or turn away from him? As we saw with Hezekiah, the question is still, What is on your heart?

One area where this testing discipline came was in the provision of life's most basic necessities: 'He humbled you, causing you to hunger and then feeding you with manna' (v. 3), which Moses says had a dual purpose. In the same verse he says that it was to teach them a vital lesson: 'that man does not live on bread alone, but on every word that comes from the mouth of the LORD.' This is not saying that bread and food have no significance. Patently they do, since people die if they do not eat. Nor is it just saying that God can provide for our needs, important though that is to remember. Rather, Moses is pointing out that God provided them with food (in this case, manna from heaven) to demonstrate that there is something higher than food that we need: the words that come from his mouth. His words, teaching, law, promises, commands, guidance, gospel—all these, and more, are not merely words. As Moses points out later in Deuteronomy (32:47), 'they are your life', the very thing that gives a true foundation to existence for all humanity. Jesus said much the same about himself in John's Gospel (chapter 6) when he fed a crowd of 5000 people with twelve loaves of bread. When they came looking for more he urged them not to look for bread that goes mouldy, but rather to look beyond the satisfaction of daily hunger and seek the true bread from heaven that would endure to eternal life. From this remark he used the opportunity to talk about himself as the bread of life that satisfies the deepest longings of the soul and brings eternal life (John 6:35). Without his words—without Jesus—we wither, so it is not to be wondered at that Western civilization is now in crisis, when for the past three centuries it has increasingly attempted to live on bread alone and has steadily squeezed the words of God out of public life altogether.

The second aim of this testing and feeding process mentioned in verse 16 was simply 'so that … it might go well with you.' We assume that hardship and testing can only have negative results, but Moses is convinced that the period in the wilderness will have had a long-term beneficial impact on those who endured it. As the writer to the Hebrews observes in Hebrews 12, 'no discipline seems pleasant at the time. Later on, however, it produces a harvest of righteousness and peace for those who have been trained by it' (v. 11). Having thus learned to trust God in the wilderness they should then hold on to God in the good times that follow.

The centre of the chapter focuses on the land and how good it will be. The picture is of overflowing abundance, where the Israelites prosper, their wealth increases and they eat and are completely satisfied. But in contrast to his review of the time in the desert, where God's provision of their needs in hardship made them see how much they needed God, Moses does not assume that this rich generosity will automatically produce rich faith; rather, just the opposite. He gives a blunt warning—do not forget the Lord—for it is at this point that faith is most under threat, whether we realize it or not. And he identifies some of the likely outcomes of living in such a prosperous environment, all of which should speak to us who are living in hot water in the West.

The first of these is straightforward forgetfulness. As we noted earlier in this book, there was real significance in the request 'give us our daily bread' since the labourer only received one day's wages at a time. But with our food surpluses, international distribution networks and long-term storage facilities, the request not merely loses a lot of its impact for us, it is also very possible that we forget that we need to make the request at all. Just as you can still find children brought up in an urban situation who have no idea what relationship a cow has to the milk they find in the supermarkets, so you will find people who are simply unaware that God has anything to do with the provision of the food they eat.

> The nation that owed its very existence to God would bite the divine hand that fed them, forget their relationship with him, disobey his laws, deny they owed him anything, and on occasions even transfer their allegiance to other gods who had done nothing for them.

But, as with all sin, forgetfulness is never as straightforward as that. The Bible tells us that there is always a moral dimension to human actions in regard to God and this is no different. There is a telling observation about this in Hosea when God says, 'When I fed them, they were satisfied; when they were satisfied, they became proud; then they forgot me' (Hosea 13:6). The appearance of that word 'pride' here and on Moses' lips (Deuteronomy 8:14) reveals that there is something more than absent-mindedness going on. In much the same way that the theory of evolution has provided a convenient way of pushing God out of science (and has been used to that effect), so men and women can use the abundance of good things as an excuse to forget God. If I have more than enough I do not need to go back to the supplier as often; in fact I may be able to leave him out altogether. I can forget that he has given me everything I have, and then conveniently ignore the obligations I have towards him, whether that is in terms of keeping 'his commands, his laws and his decrees' as Moses puts it in verse 11, or simply acknowledging him and his generosity with thankfulness. For Israel to forget God would be a feat of astonishing impudence, since it would, as Moses points out, involve forgetting all the other things God had done for them, too: the exodus from Egypt, his guidance and help through all the years in the 'vast and dreadful desert' (v. 15), and his miraculous provision of food. But they managed it. In years to come the nation that owed its very existence to God would bite the divine hand that fed them, forget their relationship with him, disobey his laws, deny they owed him anything, and on occasions even transfer their allegiance to other gods who had done nothing for them. But Moses is not so starry-eyed that he has not seen this coming. We think lottery winners are naive when they say that the ten million they have won will not change them, because we know it will, often for the worse. Moses is simply observing that hitting the jackpot can also change us for the worse in our relationship with God.

But forgetfulness of God's goodness is just the start of the problems prosperity can cause for faith. In 8:17 Moses puts his finger on what has become the defining philosophy of our materialistic, success-oriented age: 'You may say, "My power and the strength of my hands have produced this wealth for me."' We congratulate the self-made man, an icon of baby-boomer hard work and dedication, who has perhaps pulled himself up from poverty or deprivation in childhood to achieve success; but we fail to notice what the cost to him may have been. Success can breed a self-confidence and self-sufficiency that refuses to acknowledge that God has been involved at any point in the creation of wealth, when God is the one who gave the ability to produce it in the first place. It is not uncommon to hear people in the UK proclaim that they do not believe in God because they have never had any help from him. The irony of such a statement screams out from the page when placed alongside what Moses is saying: these people are living in the fourth richest nation in the world and they maintain God has done nothing for them. That is possibly to be expected from a secular mindset. Where the tragedy strikes deepest, however, is when people who have previously acknowledged their dependence upon God are so blinded by his gifts that they fail to see the Giver any longer. Moses warned that this was likely if they did not watch themselves carefully, and he was sadly proved right.

> Moses is simply observing that hitting the jackpot can also change us for the worse in our relationship with God.

Keeping the faith

Historical tradition tells us that of all the apostles John lived longest. He was apparently the only one to die peacefully in his bed, but that wasn't because the Romans hadn't tried to dispose of him. One of the tortures he was allegedly subjected to was being thrown alive into a big pot of water which was steadily heated until it was boiling. It should have killed him, but somehow it didn't. I have no idea how true that story is—it does sound a little far-fetched—but it illustrates the problem. How can we keep faith vital when the environment in which we are living is working against us so much? How can we avoid faith being shrivelled by a culture that is not merely rich, but which flaunts its wealth, promotes greed, assumes that everyone wants everything bigger and better and entices us to join the party?

If forgetfulness is the problem, the first step must be to remind ourselves continually what sort of environment we are living in. The reason the frog is boiled alive is because it grows used to the rising temperature and never thinks to ask whether it is being affected by what is going on around it and to get out while it can; but what does that mean for us? Some people have chosen the route of complete isolation from society, preferring to jump out of the water altogether before it boils, and whole movements have been founded on such sacrifice. But it is interesting that the Bible does not insist that Christians take vows of poverty or form monastic communities in order to avoid being compromised by the rich society around them. What we are called to do, however, is to ensure that we jump out of the values that our society lives by, so that we are then in a position to speak to that society and challenge its assumptions and values with the gospel. This means that we must aim to be always aware of what that society is doing to us. Living in a rich society, we can come to share its values and assume that we must have what it offers, all the while thinking that faith remains unaffected. But Jesus reminds us that it is not possible to serve both God and money (Matthew 6:24) because both demand total allegiance, so we are fooling ourselves if we think we can immerse ourselves in everything a rich culture stands for and somehow retain a strong faith.

Another step is to remember who has brought us to where we are and that we owe everything to him. The Israelites had the exodus and their experience of God's protection in the desert at this point to help them remember. By this great event God had saved them out of slavery in Egypt and taken them as his own people, and he built into their religious culture the means to remind them that they therefore belonged to him. Passover celebrations each year rehearsed the great escape and proclaimed their commitment not to forget what God had done. Sadly, however, as with the screening on British TV of Steve McQueen's escapades on a motorbike in *The Great Escape* each Christmas or New Year, these celebrations became part of the furniture, so normal that they were not noticed and their meaning was ignored. The Israelites found it all too easy to keep up the ceremony and still do just what Moses warned them against—becoming proud and forgetting God.

We have our own Passover to remember—that Jesus, our Passover, has been sacrificed for us (1 Corinthians 5:7). By his death—which he called his 'exodus' in Luke 9:31, translated as 'departure'—and resurrection he has made us his own, with the same claim over us as the Lord had over Israel. At the birth of the New Testament church in Acts 2 we are told that new Christians made a point of devoting themselves to the breaking of bread, that is, remembering Jesus and his death for sins. Looking at what business analysts might call their 'core values' in Acts 2:42 we gain a good idea of their other priorities around this: devotion to the teaching given by the apostles, to sharing the common life they had in Christ, and to prayer. All of these were designed to ensure they did not forget the key to who they were, that is, Jesus Christ, who had died for them. The moment that his death and our remembrance of it assumes the status of an empty ritual that just fills the schedule, we are in big trouble.

Lastly, the survival of faith in a prosperous environment has a lot to do with our attitude to the money we actually have. There are rich characters in the Bible who demonstrate that it is quite possible to be rich and faithful to God at the same time, if only we are careful, but the dangers are real. Paul's observation in 1 Timothy 6:9–10 is that people whose ambition is to get rich open themselves to temptation that destroys them in the end, because the love of money is the root of all kinds of evil. In saying this he probably has in mind the church leaders who were giving young Timothy such grief in his ministry: teaching false doctrines and splitting the church, they revealed what sort of men they were by their greed.

The antidote to this self-destructive grasping for more is 'godliness with contentment' (6:6). Ironically, the satisfaction that Moses speaks of as coming from being rich does not promote contentment. It may not only undermine faith by leading people to forget God, but may also lead to a greater yearning for more that in the end does not satisfy at all. We know this only too well in our society where we can see spirals of increasing consumption mirrored by decreasing contentment. Godliness, however, is different. Paul tells Timothy that it is best to be content with what we have in the Lord (and he knew from experience what it was both to be in want and to have plenty) and, if there is any fighting for more to be done, it should be for more in the way of knowing Christ and growing more like him. But he is aware that there are rich people in the church and his advice for them is significant. Firstly, don't put your hope in your wealth because it is so unreliable—and recent financial crises have demonstrated how true that still is. Rather, make sure that your hope is firmly placed in God who gives richly, and demonstrate this by being rich in good deeds, being generous and willing to share with others. Perhaps more than anything else, generosity and a willingness to share indicate where our hope really lies and that we do not share our society's values. Millionaires are more common than they used to be, but I once knew a millionaire who was among the meanest penny-pinchers I have ever encountered. He quibbled over the price of everything, asking for discounts when he bought a book of stamps and trying to avoid paying the odd pence when he filled his car up with petrol. But he was only a more extreme example of what comes naturally when money comes into the picture. Rich generosity is not a natural trait, even for Christians, but if Christians are to resist the boiling water of materialism and greed that will shrivel faith out of existence, then rich generosity is an absolute necessity. The gecko's fate awaits us if we fail.

> Rich generosity is an absolute necessity.

Summary: Faith may blossom when life is hard, but wither when life becomes easy.

Key verse: Hosea 13:6: 'When I fed them, they were satisfied; when they were satisfied, they became proud; then they forgot me.'

To think about: What practical steps are you going to take to ensure that your faith continues to grow in a prosperous environment?

'When you have eaten and are satisfied, praise the LORD your God for the good land he has given you. Be careful that you do not forget the LORD your God …', Deuteronomy 8:10–11.

'After Uzziah became powerful, his pride led to his downfall', 2 Chronicles 26:16.

Thinking more deeply

Money is certainly one of the most ensnaring and heart-changing of possessions. It seems desirable at a distance. It often proves a poison when in our hand. No man can possibly tell the effect of money on his soul, if it suddenly falls to his lot to possess it. Many an one did run well as a poor man, who forgets God when he is rich.

J.C. Ryle, *Practical Religion.*

Note

1 **Irina Ratushinskaya,** quoted in **Simon Coupland,** *Spicing up your speaking: 247 great illustrations to liven up your talks* (London: Monarch Books, 2000).

My story

A mother's reflections on a child's illness

Thomas and Wendy Smiley have worked in the Middle East since the late 1980s, raising four children in the midst of several bouts of life-threatening disease in their oldest son, Kris, who, at the time of writing, is in the recuperative stage of treatment.

'It's probably just a muscle strain, since they were practising their kicks all last week at Taekwondo, you know.' I whispered to Thomas, my husband, as we lay awake in bed one night in November 2003. But the unspoken niggling thought was in both of our minds.

We had had these niggling thoughts frequently pop up during the previous twelve years whenever our fifteen-year-old son displayed any symptom of illness. When he was a toddler he had fought and won a desperate battle with an aggressive childhood cancer, so there were most likely going to be repercussions in his body one way or another. As it turned out, the tests that December, one month later, showed that the pain was *not* a pulled muscle; it was *not* scar tissue; it was *not* an infection. It was radiation-induced (yes, from the first cancer treatment) osteosarcoma. Bone cancer.

We were on the threshold of another battle. How would we deal with it this time? We had been in our immortal twenties the first time around with two tiny kids; serious illness and death had not been in our understanding. The Lord had been gracious and compassionate, however, and he brought us through the deep valleys of pain, grief, and near-death, to an understanding of his goodness and faithfulness in the midst of it all. We had wrestled with issues of faith, such as the fact that the Lord does not punish his children with harsh diseases, although he does allow them to happen. We had been given grace to allow for mystery. We had learned to rest in the assurance that he was walking with us every step of our journey, bearing the agony with us.

But would our faith stand the test this time—and not only ours, but also that of our four very cognizant children? Would someone say something hurtful, such as, 'You know, Taekwondo has evil roots; maybe that's why your brother got cancer'? As parents, we had seriously worked that issue through the minute a well-meaning brother in Christ had mentioned his concern to us privately. But we had experienced deeply that God is good; he is for us, not against us. Giving our child cancer because he was participating in a sport is not at all consistent with who God is. We took every opportunity to share these truths as a family, and pray them into our hearts and minds.

So Kristofer's second cancer battle began in earnest the day after Christmas 2003, when he received his first round of high-dose chemo. At that time, we as a family were wrapped in God's mercy. He spoke personally to me about hope, and led my eye to any and all verses to do with hope and faith and trust. I have recorded in my journal my heart as a mother wrestling with the Lord during the time of the initial gloomy diagnosis: '… I don't know what to say or think or feel. There's no way I'm going through life without my boy, Lord. No way. Please do what you need to, but save my boy. Please. Please. Please.' And the next line of writing records what my eye fell upon in my open Bible, 'Do not be afraid, for I am with you' (Isaiah 43:5a). With obvious words straight from the Lord like these, not just once, but over and over, my hope grew. But this hope did not grow necessarily from the assurance that my son would not die—because all are appointed to die sometime—but from the assurance that my Father would be very present throughout every step of the way.

This 'very present help in trouble' (Psalm 46:1, NKJV) was vital through the ensuing periods of Kris's intense pain; when the toxic medicines had their worst effect; when we were sleep-deprived from staying up through the nights to attend to Kris's multiple needs, especially after his radical surgery to remove his tumour; when there were side-effects of the drugs that were unmanageable, and seemed worse than the cancer itself; when multiple corrective surgeries brought no relief; when the suffering all around us of the other children in the hospital threatened to overwhelm us. As one writer put it, I was 'driven from the paths of ease to storm the secret place' of God's peace in the midst of deep trouble, and his hope in the midst of despair. As I did, I began to see the good all around us: the friends who dropped everything to help drive our kids to a music lesson; the school parents bringing meals each week; the car being loaned to us for a whole year; the understanding of our kids' teachers; the kindness of the nurses. These were all brilliant rays of hope dispelling the threatening darkness.

The most brilliant of the rays came from our children, as they shared with us bits and pieces of their journey. Josiah, thirteen years old, became Kris's ally in comic relief; it seemed that no matter what was happening, the two of them could find something to laugh about. Eleven-year-old Zack took it upon himself to be a sort of butler—attending to doors being opened as Kris 'crutched' through them, bringing meals on trays up to Kris's bed, or fetching items he needed, but was too tired to get. Finally, Kris's ten-year-old sister Natali rallied her entire class to pray daily for her big brother. Parents would come up to me at school, and ask specific questions relating to Kris's health, illustrating to me how clearly Natali was explaining the prayer needs. It seemed our concerns for our children's welfare mattered greatly to their Father in heaven. He was drawing them to himself, even as Jesus did, as he 'put his hands on them and blessed them' (Mark 10:16) in the midst of great upheaval.

Kristofer himself, now as a maturing young adult of eighteen, has grappled long and hard. With questions and mysteries still resident in his soul, his anchor remains firm. He posted these thoughts on his on-line log in February 2006:

You have caused flowers to grow in my fields and you have brought new and bright colours to my head, and I rest here underneath your hands. You made all my deserts fill with gardens; you made all my ashes turn to beauty.

Hebrews 11:1. Now faith is being sure of what we hope for, and certain of what we do not see.

I ask, humbly and unashamedly, for your blessings.

As I read my young son's reflections, I am again reminded that hope is abundant. As promised, our relationships with the Lord are not weakened by circumstances, but rather made stronger. God speaks his peace that passes all understanding into our lives in ways that awe us. Yes, our faith is stretched to the breaking point; but it has only been strengthened in the process, not broken. There is hope.

Chapter 9

9 Dying:
The end of the line

Dealing with the last enemy

It is astonishing how disinterested people are in the reality of dying (John Piper, Future Grace).

Please read 2 Corinthians 4:7–5:10.

When at school I once expressed to a friend the hope that I would live until I was at least eighty years old. My friend shocked me by disagreeing. 'It gets rather boring after fifty-five,' he said, 'so I don't see much point.' He was a teenager at the time and will, like me, be in his mid-forties now (and therefore a whole sight closer to fifty-five), so I wonder just what his current views are. Perhaps he was speaking from the perspective of an angry young man whose opinions would mellow with the passage of time, yet he managed to encapsulate the despair that many feel when faced with the thought of personal decline and death.

In our mixed-up society nothing so demonstrates the hopelessness of secular philosophies as the general attitudes to illness, growing old and dying. On the one hand, people will say that they are not afraid of death, affirming that they are happy to believe that death is the end. On the other, their lifestyles betray a desperation to avoid all thoughts about death, and a despair about the meaninglessness of life that declines tragically and ends so quickly. 'Let us eat and drink, for tomorrow we die' is the saying in 1 Corinthians 15 (v. 32) with which Paul captures the emptiness of life without the hope of resurrection through Jesus Christ. He had first-century pagan Roman society in view as he wrote, but he could just as easily have been looking at the West in the twenty-first century.

But if facing death is hard for the non-Christian world, we must also admit that it is no picnic for the Christian. This is not because life is short

150 Faith in the furnace

and dangerous for us in the West, but precisely because it is not. Life in a comfortable, safe society blurs the lines between life and death which the gospel previously exploited. In the past the Christian hope spoke strongly and clearly to people who could, for instance, be swept away without a moment's notice by illness; but now we have much more control over disease and consequently there is less opportunity for the gospel to speak. People think less about faith and the afterlife if there is less chance of dying from a particular illness. More than this, life in a culture which expects, even demands, comfort and security has changed people's attitudes to suffering, illness and death. In the past, these were accepted as inevitable features of life that had to be prepared for and faced in faith. Today they are viewed as grossly unfair attacks upon our human rights that should be prevented at all costs. Christians in the West are inevitably influenced by this thinking, as much of the literature that floods out of Christian publishing houses demonstrates, frequently betraying the same panic-stricken desperation to avoid suffering as its secular counterpart. The only difference sometimes appears to be that Christians expect that, with God in their corner, he will protect them from such unfairness by answering prayer and healing them at once, because it cannot possibly be God's will that they remain ill. The consequence of this is that, when we should be thinking about how we should face what will be our greatest test of faith, we will be as unprepared to face these problems when they arise as everyone else.

Living with death

What Paul has to say in 2 Corinthians 4 is therefore highly significant. His words reveal that in his ministry as an apostle he is in fact living with death all the time. Living with death, however, is hardly the glamorous view of Christian ministry that many people feel should be projected, either now or in Paul's day. Aren't we preaching the good news of life? Don't we speak of the light of God shining into a dark world and illuminating darkened hearts? Paul's opponents reasoned that such a great work should be led by great people and accompanied by impressive deeds. Under the influence of Greek ideas, these men reasoned that people would not be impressed with a suffering Saviour or an afflicted preacher (like Paul). People needed to see success, a God who delivered the goods and showed his power, so they worked at projecting a more attractive and alluring image of themselves, believing that people would only see that the message came from God if it was appropriately glamorous. They would not be out of place in today's prosperity and health ministries whose power-dressed leaders gleam in the television spotlight like superstars, breathing out success, vigour and star-quality. You can appreciate their logic: people are not going to believe in a God who fails to deliver them from the world's problems, or accept a message about life announced by a dying man, but the logic is false. The superstar preachers (Paul calls them 'super-apostles') may think that they are helping people to find God by projecting an image of perfection, but in fact they are obscuring the message. In the same way that if you had a Ming vase on your mantelpiece people would look at that rather than ask about its contents, so their hearers were more impressed with the preachers than with God.

> We are, he says, nothing more than weak, fragile, cracked, clay pots in which the treasure of the gospel is placed.

Paul didn't need to know about Ming vases to make his point. We are, he says, nothing more than weak, fragile, cracked, clay pots in which the treasure of the gospel is placed, and it is paradoxically in this weakness that people see the power of the message more clearly. He observes that it is through this weakness that God's power is shown, not in spite of it. The cracked clay pot of human weakness allows the glory and power of the treasure within to shine out, while human strength will tend to cover it up.

It is at this point that Paul assesses his whole life and ministry in terms of living with death. His stark summary of his ministry in 4:7–10 ('hard pressed ... perplexed ... persecuted ... struck down') ends with the words that 'we always carry around in our body the death of Jesus', but he does not use the usual word for death in this phrase. 'Dying' would be a more accurate translation, since it is a word that describes the process of dying rather than just the end of life. 'Look at me,' says Paul. 'My life and ministry reflect the dying agonies of Jesus on the cross. I am preaching the wonderful news of God's salvation at the same time as suffering so severely that my life appears outwardly to be the opposite of my message. Death is at work in me even while I am speaking about life.' It is this series of admissions that enables him to speak to us so clearly and help us face our own inevitable decline.

We do not lose heart

While she was alive Elisabeth Kübler-Ross was regarded as one of the world's principal authorities on death and dying, with her research contributing to an understanding of the process of dying and the way it affects sufferers, and her work promoting the hospice movement. Her best-known book, *On Death and Dying*, outlined five stages that she saw in a person's response to being told they had a terminal illness: starting with denial, a person will move to anger when the truth dawns on them, then bargaining to try to escape the consequences, depression when they realize that they cannot do so, finally ending with acceptance that brings a measure of peace with it. These stages were written without any overt Christian focus, although they do describe what many Christians will also experience when the Grim Reaper makes his entrance. Disbelief focuses around why God should allow this to happen and asking what good can come out of this, while bargaining takes the form of confessing unknown sins in the hope that they will hit the right one for God to forgive them and give them a stay of execution. Along with many of the early Christians, Paul, however, appears to have managed to short-circuit this process completely, since he leaps straight to an acceptance of decline and death when he says 'we do not lose heart' (v. 16).

What gives Paul the ability to do this is his understanding of the resurrection of Jesus and what it means for us. He immediately follows his brutally honest assessment of his living death in 2 Corinthians 4:7–12 with a statement that his faith is still strong—did he wonder whether his readers might think his faith was wavering?—because he knows that all is not lost. 'We know that the one who raised the Lord Jesus from the dead will also raise us with Jesus and present us with you in his presence' (4:14). This, quite simply, changes everything and sparks the remark that 'we do not lose heart' when facing rejection, hardship and death either in Christian work or in everyday life.

Living with decline

The circumstance that causes some of the most significant distress is the process that Paul identifies as 'wasting away' (v. 16). The root of this word can be found in 1 Corinthians 15:42 where Paul describes the body as 'perishable' (and we know what that means for foodstuffs). The word here is an intensification of that term and therefore graphically pictures a process by which we rot away slowly, and this is probably the part most of us fear more than anything else. It was the twentieth-century entertainer Maurice Chevalier who joked that old age isn't so bad when you consider the alternatives, but that doesn't actually make growing old any easier, other than possibly injecting a note of humour into it. It basically makes it the lesser of two evils that only postpones the greater for a few decades. Our culture tries not to think about death, so has consequently become obsessed with the fear of growing old—watch evening television and it will not be long before you are confronted by a commercial which will assure you, by using models in their early twenties and dazzlingly long scientific terms, that the cream offered will combat the signs of ageing. In fact, the films that these commercials interrupt will also be populated by people whose looks bear no relationship to their age, because the demands of Hollywood are such that movie stars—particularly women—have to look youthful or their careers on screen will come to an abrupt end. Nobody wants to grow old, Christians included, but the answer is not to pursue eternal youth, for that leads to the shallow, empty existence we can see all too clearly in the West. The answer is to pursue the inward renewal in Christ that Paul says is working in his life alongside his physical decline.

> Nobody wants to grow old, Christians included, but the answer is not to pursue eternal youth.

On more than one occasion Paul describes the Christian life in terms of a process of continual renewal. 'You have taken off your old self ... and have put on the new self, which is being renewed in knowledge in the image of its Creator' is the way he puts it in Colossians 3:9–10. Conversion to Christ is a dramatic change, putting off the old and putting on the new, but change does not stop there. The new self continues to develop in Christ, growing to know him more deeply and then seeing that knowledge work out in Christlike character. The sentence quoted above comes in the middle of a long section that begins with a list of traits that the new self in Christ will avoid (immorality, rage, lies, and so on) and concludes with those that it will strive to put into practice (compassion, gentleness, forgiveness and love). In Romans 12:2 Paul urges Christians to ensure that they continually refuse to be squeezed into the pattern of both the thinking and the behaviour of the society in which they live, and that they go on being transformed as their thinking is renewed. The presence of these exhortations in New Testament letters not only tells us how necessary it is to persevere with this aspect of Christian growth, it also indicates that this process will not come to an end this side of heaven. Renewal is a constant, daily process that is a counterbalance to the similarly slow process of physical decline.

> The Christian hope that enables us to deal with decline and death centres around being raised to eternal life with Jesus.

It is easy to see now why our society is so paranoid about ageing: people are growing old without being inwardly renewed at the same time, so it really is hopeless. Despair or anger are quite logical when the situation is viewed from this angle, for death not only strips you of life at the end, it takes away little pieces long before it finally arrives. Writer and poet Dylan Thomas voiced quite natural feelings when he wrote:

Do not go gentle into that good night,
Old age should burn and rave at close of day;
Rage, rage against the dying of the light.[1]

And the scorn that Philip Pullman, author of the prize-winning *His Dark Materials* trilogy of stories for children, pours onto C.S. Lewis's *Narnia* chronicles because of (among other things) the way they end, is consistent with his worldview. As an atheist he faces the ultimate loss of everything he has worked for at the hands of death, so it is quite understandable that he should seethe against a book that presents the death of its principal characters in a positive light.

Mention there of the *Narnia* chronicles' ending reminds us that there is more to living with decline and death than expecting personal growth. After all, it could be argued that there is not much point in being renewed throughout life if it all comes to nothing at the end. The reason we have hope in the face of these terrors is expressed in the verse mentioned earlier that changes everything: that the one who raised Jesus will raise us, too, a concept that takes us beyond the confines of this present life (v. 14).

Living with eternity

The Christian hope that enables us to deal with decline and death centres around being raised to eternal life with Jesus, but a Christian friend of mine once admitted that he could not imagine what heaven would be like and so found it almost impossible to be motivated by the prospect of going there. In his defence it must be said that the Bible gives little in the way of concrete detail about heaven, but there should still be enough information to know that it is, as Paul puts it in Philippians, far better.

> Our troubles are like so much fluff and dust, because heaven on the other side massively outweighs them all.

The first aspect that Paul focuses on in 2 Corinthians is that heaven simply outweighs the troubles we experience here, which Paul describes as 'light and momentary' (4:17). In human terms Paul's sufferings were anything but light if the summary provided in chapter 11 of 2 Corinthians is anything to go by. And they were hardly momentary, either, since Paul was persecuted virtually from the start of his Christian experience until his life was cut short (literally!) some twenty years later by a Roman executioner. So he is certainly not trivializing human suffering when he makes this remark. But Paul says that, when placed alongside the glory that awaits those who know Jesus Christ, these troubles pale into insignificance (in Romans 8:18 he observes that they are not even worth comparing with this heavenly glory), because that glory is so much weightier. Brought up on the Hebrew Scriptures, Paul would have been aware that the Hebrew word for glory is the word 'heavy', so he brings this into the Greek in which he is writing. When placed on one side of the scales our troubles are like so much fluff and dust, because heaven on the other side massively outweighs them all. In fact, the sufferings actually contribute to that glory as God rewards those who have stood firm in faith through difficult times.

This is an interesting reversal of expectations. For most people, this world is more substantial than the next and they cling to it desperately. Heaven is usually portrayed as disembodied spirits floating around, sitting on clouds and looking slightly bored, a ghostly existence that has no solidity to it. Seen that way, life on earth is far more exciting and real, and troubles far more significant. But Paul insists that appearances are deceptive and that heaven is the more real existence. What we see around us is just temporary, but the unseen glory of heaven is eternal. But there are some people who realize that life in this world is short-lived and are deeply troubled by the insecurity it causes. Those with a philosophical frame of mind would agree with the writer of Ecclesiastes in the Old Testament in his cry that 'Everything is meaningless' (1:2) because life is just like a vapour or mist that melts away. Paul also agrees with this assessment, but far from being a source of existential angst, this fact reinforces his faith. Heaven is far more real and solid than anything life down here can offer, something that becomes clearer as he speaks about heaven itself in 2 Corinthians 5.

> Heaven is far more real and solid than anything life down here can offer.

In 2 Corinthians 5 we come across the second way in which Paul's words help us handle decline and death: they force us to look at what heaven actually entails. One of the Bible's enduring metaphors for human life is to compare it to living in a tent. The Old Testament patriarchs lived in tents and had no permanent home. John describes Jesus' coming to dwell on earth as a man by using a term that means he lived among us as in a tent. And Paul now continues this metaphor by speaking of what happens when the frail tent of human life collapses. 'We have a building from God, an eternal house in heaven, not built by human hands,' he says. Once again, heaven is far more solid, more substantial and secure than anything we might find here on earth, and this contrast shows it up just about as clearly as is possible. Life on earth has no foundation, much though many try to pretend it has. However hard we hammer them in, the tent pegs of life come out one by one as we get older and, sooner or later, the tent is uprooted and the body dies. Life in heaven, however, is a solid building, a house made by God that cannot be destroyed. Paul no doubt intended this picture here to complement what he had already written in his first letter to the Corinthian church about the resurrection body, where he had written to counter those who were saying that the body would not be raised. This second letter adds more detail and would have put an end to Greek notions that the body counted for nothing by saying that the body given us in heaven would be more permanent than anything given us here on earth. In an interesting extension of this metaphor, the writer to the Hebrews says that Abraham lived as an alien in the promised land, in tents rather than building a city. He did this because he was looking ahead to his reward, which was something more substantial, 'a city with foundations whose architect and builder is God' (Hebrews 11:10). At every turn the Bible tells us that we will find no security in this life, but must rather seek it in the life to come.

> However hard we hammer them in, the tent pegs of life come out one by one as we get older and, sooner or later, the tent is uprooted and the body dies.

Not that this is easy. While it is not entirely clear what Paul means in 5:3–4 when he says that we do not want to be found 'naked' and 'unclothed', what is clear is that the dominant feature of life as tent-dwellers is that 'we groan' while waiting for the great change to take place. Life with all its insecurities is painful and frightening, even for Christians. The protracted process of wasting away is distressing and debilitating, and the struggles we feel as we grow old mirror what Paul is describing here. But this should strengthen faith, rather than weaken it. Gripped with an awareness of our own mortality we should long even more for the time when, as Paul says, we are 'clothed with our heavenly dwelling, so that what is mortal [is] swallowed up by life.' The insidious presence of death as it eats away slowly at us should be a constant reminder that this life is not heaven, and should make us yearn all the more for a time when we are free from death. That freedom is promised us in Christ, a wonderful moment when he transforms the Christian's lowly body to be like his glorious body, when he reclothes our frail exterior with something permanent, when that which is mortal is swallowed up by life. But all this will not take place until we pass into eternity. In the meantime we must groan.

But at least the Christian's struggles have a goal. This longing for something more substantial than what this life offers is a feature of human existence around the world, but in Western society it has turned people inwards. Not having a reference point of faith in God, these longings have been used to try to make this world a heaven on earth, without reference to eternity or knowing God. Western postmodern culture makes a religion out of the quest for personal self-fulfilment, so many of the longings of twenty-somethings in the twenty-first century revolve around making sure they have a good time. Decline and death, however, pull the rug from under this philosophy, because they limit the good time that can be had. To a generation soaked in its own desire to have fun, this deadly duo seems like a cruel joke because, in the end, they ruin the good time altogether and the heaven people have attempted to construct comes tumbling down. The result is an emptiness that the next thrill cannot completely fill, and a sense of futility and aimlessness that nothing fully answers.

In the meantime we must groan.

Fixing on eternity

If society's mistake is to forget eternity, you must make every effort to ensure you think about it a lot more—as Paul says, you must 'fix your eyes on what is unseen.' Film-maker and comedian Woody Allen, whose humour often revolves around death, once remarked, 'It's not that I'm afraid to die. I just don't want to be there when it happens.' We all know what he is talking about since no one relishes the prospect of falling ill, becoming increasingly debilitated, losing faculties or suffering pain. Most would probably rather just slip away quietly. But some would say the wish is misguided since it prevents us from focusing on heaven. In what was his last illness, preacher Martyn Lloyd-Jones spoke about facing terminal illness:

I am grateful to God that I have been given this time … We do not give enough time to death and our going on … We are too busy. We allow life and its circumstances so to occupy us that we do not stop and think … People say about sudden death, 'It is a wonderful way to go'. I have come to the conclusion that is quite wrong. I think the way we go out of this world is very important and this is my great desire now that I may perhaps be enabled to bear a greater testimony than before. [2]

James Casson was a family doctor who wrote about the experience of facing a terminal illness before he succumbed to cancer at the age of just thirty-seven. The booklet he produced is a mixture of personal testimony and advice which doesn't hide his distress at what he faced, but approaches the whole matter from a Christian perspective. Its title captures the Christian way of looking at this subject: *Dying—The Greatest Adventure of My Life*. But it is only possible to agree with the book's sentiment if you focus on heaven.

> This is not home and many of our problems stem from the fact that we are too comfortable to remember it.

C.S. Lewis, writing more generally about suffering, makes the following observation about the way it constrains us to readjust our focus:

The Christian doctrine of suffering explains, I believe, a very curious fact about the world we live in. The settled happiness and security which we all desire, God withholds from us by the very nature of the world: but joy, pleasure, and merriment, he has scattered broadcast. It is not hard to see why. The security we crave would teach us to rest our hearts in this world … a few moments of happy love, a landscape, a symphony, a merry meeting with our friends, a bathe or a football match, have no such tendency. Our Father refreshes us on the journey with some pleasant times, but will not encourage us to mistake them for home. [3]

This is not home and many of our problems stem from the fact that we are too comfortable to remember it, even though the Bible has many other analogies which reinforce this conviction. It tells us that we are strangers in an alien land; we are citizens of another country and our true citizenship is in heaven; we are pilgrims on a journey and find no permanent resting place here; we are betrothed to Jesus Christ, but his wedding feast will not take place until he takes us to be with him; this world we live in will not endure but will be replaced by new heavens and a new earth; our ultimate allegiance is to no earthly ruler, instead we wait for a King from heaven to rule over us; this world is temporary, while heaven is eternal; we are in the world, but we do not belong to it.

Fixing your eyes on eternity must begin with this realization: your real home is not here, but in eternity. You may not be able to say what it will look like (so I do have some sympathies for my friend with his difficulties, and if you ask any youth group what they believe about heaven you will quickly discover that he is not alone), but you do have enough information to know that it is where you really belong. At the end of *Homage to Catalonia*, George Orwell describes returning home after being wounded while fighting in the Spanish Civil War with the International Brigade. His train journey home takes him through southern England with its familiar streets and gardens and, among other things, milk standing on the doorstep. This description provides a reassuring picture of things returning to normality, a sensation that is associated with coming home. It is the same feeling when you return from holiday. It doesn't matter how good the holiday has been, there is always something deeply comforting about coming home. Whether it is the familiarity of the locality, your own house, having friends and family around, or—for the English!—just being able to get a decent cup of tea, the sensation is one of returning to the familiar, where you fit in and just feel right. At the end of his paraphrase of Psalm 23, Isaac Watts describes what it means to dwell in God's house and thus captures perfectly this same feeling in relation to heaven:

> Your real home is not here, but in eternity.

There would I find a settled rest, while others go and come,
No more a stranger or a guest, but like a child at home.4

'Home' is a significant metaphor to use. Many people picture death as setting out on a great journey into the unknown, but the Christian faith reverses the picture. This life is the hazardous journey, unpredictable and unknown; dying in Christ is coming home. It is to return to the place where you really belong, where you can be completely at peace, not because its sights, sounds and smells are familiar—they are unknown at present—but because you will be at home with God.

The great promise that runs through Scripture is that God will live with his people. In the Old Testament God resided first in the tent of meeting and then in the temple, concealed from them by layers of stone and curtaining, but among them nevertheless. When the Jews were scattered across the Middle East at the beginning of the sixth century B.C. many adopted the practice of praying towards the temple in Jerusalem in recognition of God's presence there. The exile in Babylon was an exile from God's presence, so it was revolutionary for Ezekiel, languishing in a refugee camp a thousand miles from Jerusalem, to have a vision of God's throne on wheels. God was not distant, but had turned up to be with them. In the New Testament the promise is given a deeper meaning by Jesus when he sent his Holy Spirit. The Spirit not only brings the presence of Jesus into our midst wherever we are (and where just two or three come together in his name) so that we can say Jesus is with us at all times, he also brings Jesus to live in us. No longer located in a city, or even a building, he takes up residence within those who have faith in him, so they can never be separated from him, even though they may feel it at times. Heaven brings these strands together with the great statement found in Revelation 21:3 which pictures the culmination of world history with a new heaven and a new earth replacing the old: 'Now the dwelling of God is with men, and he will live with them. They will be his people, and God himself will be with

> This life is the hazardous journey, unpredictable and unknown; dying in Christ is coming home.

them and be their God.' The description that follows in subsequent chapters is one of absolute security in the city where God dwells, with nothing separating God from his people and face-to-face contact that will never be broken. The very next verse puts its effect succinctly and beautifully: 'He will wipe every tear from their eyes. There will be no more death or mourning or crying or pain, for the old order of things has passed away.'

There is probably no better way of describing the solid comfort that heaven provides and therefore that fixing your mind on it will bring, for this verse pictures that deep-seated longing that everyone of us has for acceptance, security, and somewhere to belong to, be known and be loved. To go to heaven is, to use the language of previous generations, to go home.

It is this that transforms the very human dilemma of growing old and dying, injecting a note to the experience that none of our secular philosophies can hope to match. That note is one of confidence, which Paul mentions in 2 Corinthians 5:6 when he says quite boldly 'we are always confident …' Confidence is not the usual word associated with this phase of human experience, because we tend to associate it with pride and self-reliance. But it is nothing more than taking God at his word and standing on the evidence he gives us. Since God has raised Jesus, he will raise us also. An awareness of salvation, heaven, a relationship with the living God, the promise of being raised into God's presence with the family of God—all these lift the Christian's experience beyond the rather bleak and hopeless prospect of wasting away slowly, and clothe it with peace and even joy. Death has become nothing more dangerous than moving to a bigger house: stressful at the time, but soon forgotten when the boxes are unpacked.

Summary: When death is at work in us, God's life shines out more clearly.

Key verses: 2 Corinthians 4:16–18: 'We do not lose heart. Though outwardly we are wasting away, yet inwardly we are being renewed day by day. For our light and momentary troubles are achieving for us an eternal glory that far outweighs them all. So we fix our eyes not on what is seen, but on what is unseen. For what is seen is temporary, but what is unseen is eternal.'

To think about: How can you fix your eyes more on heaven and eternity in a society that is so focused on the here and now?

'Just as the sufferings of Christ flow over into our lives, so also through Christ our comfort overflows', 2 Corinthians 1:5.

'I desire to depart and be with Christ, which is better by far', Philippians 1:23.

'Our citizenship is in heaven', Philippians 3:20.

Thinking more deeply

Picture two skydivers. They are both free-falling. Their speed is the same. They both seem to be free … But there is one crucial difference: only one of them has a parachute. Does this change the sense of freedom that they enjoy? Yes. Both are free to fall with gravity, but only one of them is free not to. The other is a slave to gravity and gravity will kill him in the end. If he can somehow deny that he has no parachute he might be able to have an exhilarating experience. But if he realizes he is doomed, he will be enslaved through fear during his entire fall, and all the joy of this so-called freedom will vanish. He must either deny the reality (which will mean slavery to illusion), or succumb to fear (which will mean slavery to terror), or be rescued by someone with a parachute. So it is in the world. Apart from Christ, we are subject to slavery all our lives through fear of death.

John Piper, *Future Grace*.

When the famous agnostic Robert Ingersoll died, the printed funeral order of service left this solemn instruction, 'There will be no singing.' Few people feel like singing in the face of death.

Max Lucado, *Six Hours one Friday*.

But if God aims by suffering to detach us from this world it is because he has a greater goal for us in view. Slum clearance is not an end in itself, simply to satisfy the town planners, its ultimate aim is to move people to better homes. So in all God's dealings, which may at times appear harsh, he is gently and graciously preparing us for removal.

Herbert Carson, *Facing Suffering*.

Note

1 **Dylan Thomas,** *Do Not Go Gentle Into That Good Night* (1951).
2 **Murray,** *David Martyn Lloyd-Jones*, p. 730.
3 **C.S. Lewis,** *The Problem of Pain* (London: Fount Paperbacks, 1979), p. 103.
4 **Isaac Watts,** 'My Shepherd will supply my need'.

My story

Losing a daughter

Merle and Gloria Inniger served as missionaries in Pakistan from the 1950s, but here Merle writes about one event in their retirement, the loss of their daughter.

It was not the phone call we had hoped for. My wife, Gloria, and I had planned one of our ministry trips to India from early December 1999 until March or April of 2000, timing it to coincide with the birth of our daughter Amy Jo's first child in New Delhi. With her husband, David Boone, Amy Jo was living in Shri Nawas Puri, a poor section of the city, where for two years they had been following what they believed was God's call to teach and bring the good news to people in that place, living, learning and sharing with them in their struggles and joys. Earlier in that year she had learned that she was pregnant. She and David were overjoyed. It was what they had prayed and waited for after five years of marriage. Now, however, on that dreary November day, the call came that the severe headaches that Amy Jo had suffered for about a month were not pregnancy related, but were the result of a fast-growing brain tumour.

Our early years in Pakistan—we had been evangelistic and teaching missionaries there since the mid 1950s—were not times of unusual testing. Yes, there were difficult times—unfulfilled desire for a family, occasional shortage of missionary allocations, misunderstanding of our message by Muslims, problems in establishing a church … But we did not see these as especially heavy trials such as Job had to bear. Amy Jo had been a special gift from the Lord during this period. We had two children, Jim and Laura, who came into our family by adoption. We were led to believe that we might never have children born to us. Nevertheless, in the nineteenth year of our married life Amy Jo was born, a total surprise! Our days in South Asia as a family were happy times.

As years went on, the Lord brought more purposeful trials and suffering into our lives. As we studied the lives of his people in Scripture we became aware of God's purpose through suffering, which has as its end the purifying and sanctifying of the saints. This way is certainly different for everyone, but there are principles clearly taught in Scripture which apply to each one called to follow the Lord Jesus Christ.

To give details of what this meant for us is clearly impossible. It involved a ministry of travelling and living for periods of time in South Asia in our retirement years (since 1993), to go where we were needed to teach the Bible in Urdu, to fill in for someone on leave, to encourage national pastors and so on. This ministry, however, was in much weakness. I am genetically very susceptible to cancer and, during this era of ministry trips, I have had to cope with four types of cancer which would show up at the most unexpected places and times. For instance, one cancer was not detected by doctors in India and was finally treated successfully by surgery in a hospital in Pakistan in September 1993. There were other periods of pain when there was a temptation to discouragement, and yet relief was always provided, encouraging us on in our ministry.

But nothing compared to the heaviness of the news of Amy Jo's brain tumour at the time of the expected delivery of her first child. Thousands in many places were praying for a miracle of healing. We arrived in Delhi in time to stand at the bedside of a dying daughter and to try to comfort a grieving husband. She had survived her brain surgery and the delivery of a daughter by caesarean section. Then she was conscious for just a few hours to hold her baby and speak to her, before she slipped away. Her suffering has touched and blessed many lives.

Are such things accidents? Are such tragedies arbitrary? We do not believe they are.

The Scriptures from God's inspired Word which were used by the Holy Spirit to guide us, teach us and encourage us were, among others: Isaiah 53; Matthew 18:5–17; 1 Peter 1:3–9; Romans 8, especially verses 12–39. We cannot expound and explain here how these Scriptures have taught and edified us, so we will make just a few remarks about the main things we have learned.

Isaiah 53 describes the purposes of the Lord Almighty in the sufferings of our Lord Jesus Christ. His sufferings are the lodestar for us in this world of woe. Why did he suffer? Isaiah 53:10 gives the amazing word, 'Yet it was the LORD's will to crush him and cause him to suffer.' It was so ordained for our sakes, because 'he was pierced for our transgressions, he was crushed for our iniquities' (53:5). That is the main purpose. Yet there was more. Verse 4 says, 'he took up our infirmities and carried our sorrows.' This assures us that as we carry this mortal world's load of sickness, sorrows and heavy burdens, he is right there with us! This thought in itself eases our burden and gives us tremendous comfort: 'Jesus is here; he is sharing my load. I can rest in him.'

So there is both redemptive and exemplary power in the cross of our Lord Jesus Christ. We live and die by that! And just now, as our trips are on hold because of prostate cancer, we yield our days, weeks and months totally to him. His love holds us fast.

Merle went to be with the Lord on 24 April 2006.

Part 3
Fighting the fire—help is at hand

10 Strengthening:
Power in your corner

Finding help in need

Christ departed scattering promises of power (Charles Williams[1]).

Please read 2 Corinthians 1:1–11, Hebrews 4:14–16 and John 14:15–31.

'More tea, vicar?' No phrase captures more effectively what people think ministers in Britain do for a living and at the same time dismisses their work as irrelevant. What can be easier and more useless than taking tea with elderly members of the congregation, all the while listening to their gripes about declining health? I don't know that many people hold that rather cynical view of the minister's work, but tea and sympathy has become a byword for a well-meaning but futile attempt at rendering assistance. Unable to do anything concrete to alleviate the situation, the hapless minister is reduced to sighing while holding the sufferer's hand.

> It isn't an exam that we pass or fail, so much as a new experience of God and his grace.

That caricature is helpful in only one respect: in that it reminds us that the difficult circumstances we have been considering in the previous chapters require more than comforting words to get us through. We need God's help, but we may be reluctant to ask. It is possible to conclude (wrongly) that, because God is the one who sends testing circumstances our way, he will not help us in them. After all, a teacher who sets an exam doesn't give the answers to the pupils who have to take it, so why should God help us cheat? But that is to fail to understand the nature of God's testing. It isn't an exam that we pass or fail, so much as a new experience of God and his grace. If anything, it is designed to put us in circumstances where we have to call on him because we have appreciated in a new way that we are unable to get through without his aid. Fortunately, such help is readily available and we only have to ask.

Powerful sympathy

If you were to read only the Acts accounts of Paul's life (and read them superficially) it might be possible to believe that Paul was a hard-headed trailblazer who pushed through opposition completely undaunted, simply because most of us have the notion in our heads that this is what pioneers are like. Some missionary biographies, for instance, read like an instalment of the action-packed *Boy's Own* comics my father's generation used to read as children, where the hero emerges victorious against overwhelming odds and doesn't even have to comb his hair. But Paul's second letter to the Corinthian church blows such fanciful notions away altogether, as Paul opens his heart to us more than at any other time and reveals both the extent of his suffering for the gospel and the depth of his feelings about such suffering.

We noted in chapter 7 that in 2 Corinthians 1:3–11 Paul tells us that when he visited the province of Asia he experienced some of the most difficult circumstances he had ever faced. The pressure, he said 'was far beyond our ability to endure, so that we despaired even of life' (1:8). While we are not certain which incident he is talking about, we do know what he learned about God in it. We looked at the way the whole incident brought him to rely on God more, rather than on his own abilities, but Paul also comments about the new experience he had of God in the trauma. His opening statement gives us the details where he calls God 'the Father of compassion and the God of all comfort' (1:3). The first term refers to pity for the sufferings of others, a genuine fellow-feeling for their ills and troubles, and tells us that God's compassion flows to us when we are under great trials. This is a clear reminder of what the Old Testament teaches in Psalm 103:13–14: 'As a father has compassion on his children, so the LORD has compassion on those who fear him, for he knows how we are formed, he remembers that we are dust.' The second term is perhaps even more significant, since it also indicates the practical action that God takes: 'the God of all comfort'. The English word 'comfort' is significant in itself, since its root concerns the giving of strength, but the original Greek verb is even more helpful. Its basic meaning is to stand alongside someone to give encouragement, and Paul uses the term no fewer than nine times in verses 3 to 7 to leave us in no doubt about God's comfort for his suffering people. We will see that a related word is also used to describe the work of Jesus and the Holy Spirit for us, but even if that extra evidence were not available, we would still have a wonderful picture. God in compassion draws alongside us in our need in order to give strength and encouragement. There is nothing, however desperate, that can separate us from him and his tender care. Whatever arises, his comfort is everything we need, because he stands with us to give us the help we require.

> Whatever arises, his comfort is everything we need, because he stands with us to give us the help we require.

God is frequently charged with either being unable to help ('I'd love to do something to sort out the mess you guys are in, but right now I've got it all on to deal with the wars around the world, so I'm afraid you'll have to wait') or being unwilling because he is callously indifferent to our plight ('Sure I could help, but I just can't be bothered'); but this short phrase in 1:3 debunks these ideas immediately. He is neither powerless nor uncaring. Of course, if you expect God to show his care and prove his power by shielding you from all troubles, then you are going to be disappointed. Accidents happen, natural disasters sweep away the innocent, people succumb to illness, others get away with murder, and the world hates God and his Son and so persecutes their followers. God has never indicated that he will spare us from the consequences of living in an evil world, but he has promised to provide help to those under such circumstances and Paul discovered this to be true when he stared death in the face.

We don't know what it was that brought him to the point that he felt the end was near, but it was in this that he experienced a new awareness of God. Far from feeling abandoned, it was here that he was aware of

God standing alongside him to strengthen him. This sounds very subjective to the outside observer—and it is hard to describe—but that does not make it imaginary. It could perhaps best be described as the sensation of being carried through, so that instead of blind panic there is a calm resolve and even a quiet confidence. A few days prior to writing this my wife and I learned of the sudden death of a Christian friend, who had suffered a heart attack while praying and reading the Scriptures. The letter from this friend's husband informing us of her death breathes out a heavenly peace that defies explanation in anything other than Christian terms. It isn't natural, as anyone who has to deal with grief will tell you, and the husband in essence would agree. He has stated that he is amazed at the strength God has given him to cope, not just with the trauma of finding her dead, but with everything else that follows such a bereavement. Paul describes that upholding in Philippians 4:6–7 where he instructs his readers not to be 'anxious about anything, but in everything, by prayer and petition, with thanksgiving, [to] present your requests to God. And the peace of God, which transcends all understanding, will guard your hearts and your minds in Christ Jesus.' That puts it so well and explains why such peace is so hard to explain: it is beyond understanding. Yet it is real and comes in such a way that it literally garrisons the heart and mind and sets a guard against forces that normally destabilize a person, demonstrating that God is neither distant and powerless nor cold and uncaring.

> It literally garrisons the heart and mind and sets a guard against forces that normally destabilize a person.

More than this, Paul also found God's help to extricate him from the situation and save his life. Once again, we do not know the details behind this account, but what he tells us is enough. When God stood near Paul he delivered him from the danger he was in. It sounds like it was touch and go ('in our hearts we felt the sentence of death', v. 9) but God stepped in at just the right time and in such a way as to make it clear that only he could have done this. Any reading of Christian biographies, church history or accounts of the spread of the church across the world will reveal that timely deliverance is one of God's specialities, when he snatches victory from the jaws of defeat. The turn-around is sometimes so unexpected that the only adequate way of describing this is to say that he 'raises the dead' and that is certainly how it seemed to Paul on this occasion (v. 9). But it gave him confidence to trust in God and believe that this assistance would be available in the future.

If we are to withstand similar circumstances that come our way, we are going to have to hold fast to this idea that God is one who raises the dead. If all our best-laid plans seem to crumble before our eyes, then we need to realize that God often arranges events to bring us to see this form of resurrection first-hand. And then, like Paul, we will come to appreciate that it is God's power that we need and can ask for in the future (and note in 1:11 that we can ask on behalf of others that they will receive it, too).

A friend in need

In the story of Aladdin the young hero is betrayed and locked in a cave, but is saved when he discovers a tatty old lamp that releases a genie when rubbed. Granted three wishes, Aladdin is able to escape, become rich and eventually marry the princess. It would be interesting to discover how many people reject God because they realize that genies exist only in fairy stories and they think that this is what the church is saying God is like. A genie is a being with absolute power who is enslaved to the owner of the lamp he is trapped in and who must obey the owner's orders without question or hesitation. In the Disney animation of the story the genie's entrance is the cue for a song promising Aladdin anything he wants, but it adds a more human touch to the usual picture of a genie that has no feeling for its master by concluding with the words, 'You ain't never had a friend like me!' Needless to say, even that brings us no closer to the Bible's description of our relationship with God, for God is not a genie at our disposal and he will never be enslaved to us. But he does call us his friends, which should make us certain that he will draw alongside us when we call and give us the help we need when we ask.

> Timely deliverance is one of God's specialities.

It is not only the Father who does this for us. The noun related to the verb translated 'comfort' that we encountered earlier is used in 1 John 2:1 to describe what the Lord Jesus does: 'if anybody does sin, we have one who speaks to the Father in our defence—Jesus Christ, the Righteous One.' The word initially referred to a defence counsellor in a court of justice or an advocate (readers brought up on older versions of the Bible will recall that they use this one word 'advocate' for the NIV's phrase), and then was applied more widely to a person who pleaded someone else's cause, acted as an intercessor on their behalf, or even just stood with them to give moral support. It is in this context that John speaks of Jesus standing by us, defending us—not from the Father, for it was the Father who sent him to save us, but as our Saviour representing us in God's presence so that our continuing sins do not separate us from him.

This ministry of intercession is described more fully in Hebrews 4:14–16 where the writer begins to talk about Jesus as our great high priest. The danger his readers were facing was of drifting from the faith when under pressure to return to their Jewish religious traditions, so the writer is endeavouring to demonstrate that Jesus is superior to everything they have ever known. At this point, he is urging them to hold fast to the faith because Jesus is more effective as a priest than any who had served in the temple, since he does not minister on earth, but has 'gone through the heavens' (v. 14) and is therefore able to represent us before God himself. But in case his readers are in danger of feeling that Jesus is too removed from human experience to represent us adequately, he gives them the vital reminder that we have a high priest who understands us completely.

It is not uncommon for people to think of Jesus as so great and remote that he cannot possibly understand how we feel. While on holiday in Brittany in northern France one summer I visited several churches known for a particular architectural feature known as the 'parish close'. One of them had a plaque above the tomb of a local saint urging the faithful to pray to God through this man because he had been a lawyer (in French, an advocate) and during his lifetime had spoken out for the poor, representing them before the local feudal lords. Even though it is wrong, it is easy to see the logic: because this man experienced human life to the full, he will be able to understand the struggles you face, and since he spent his life helping the needy, he will be open for business today and will be perfectly happy to have you come to him now. Apart from the unbiblical notion of praying to fellow sinners who died hundreds of years ago, it is wrong because it is suggesting, at least indirectly, that Jesus does not understand us fully and that he is not approachable, so that a medieval corpse is better fitted to intercede for us than the Son of God who rose from the dead and lives today.

Thankfully the writer to the Hebrews dispels that one immediately. Jesus is able to sympathize with us in our weaknesses, not because he shares those weaknesses (which are caused by sin), but because he has been tempted—in every way—just as we are. Since he was fully human (Hebrews 2:17 says he was 'made like his brothers in every way') he faced the same temptations as we do and suffered as he resisted them to the point of death. The writer's observation in 2:17 is that it was necessary for Jesus to share our human experience if he was to be a 'merciful and faithful high priest' and 'make atonement for the sins of the people', but it was also essential that he resist completely the sin that defeats us so that he could then help us. So in Hebrews 4:15 the writer adds the necessary brief comment that, while he faced our temptations, he did so without succumbing to them and remained 'without sin.' It is this combination of his experience of sin's power and his sinless purity that fits Jesus perfectly to help us, and the writer urges us to make the most of the benefits this offers.

'Approach the throne of grace with confidence' is the way he puts it in verse 16. You have one who has made atonement for your sins, so you will 'receive mercy', but because he has also shared your experience of the evil influence of temptation you will 'find grace to help [you] in [your] time of need.' In fact, because Jesus did not cave in under the pressure of temptation, you will find more help than anyone else can give, since he has faced its fiercest attacks. Once again there is deep comfort here for saints who feel they are being tested and tried beyond the limits of their endurance. Jesus understands the unbearable pressures we are facing and so draws alongside us to bring the help that we need to stand firm. He does not automatically reduce the pressure (the rest of the letter to the Hebrews makes that abundantly clear), but he urges us to draw strength from him, the great high priest who perfectly meets our need.

Inner strength from a divine Helper

We can round off this description of Trinitarian assistance by looking at what is said about the work of the Holy Spirit. In John 14 Jesus begins to speak about sending the Holy Spirit who will assist the disciples once Jesus has been taken from them, so in 14:16 he says that the Father 'will give you another Counsellor to be with you for ever—the Spirit of truth.'

It is that word 'Counsellor' that is of particular interest to us. We met it in 1 John 2 where it was used to describe Jesus speaking on our behalf before the Father when we sin, and the related word was in 2 Corinthians 1 speaking of the comfort the Father gives in extreme circumstances (hence some versions translate it 'Comforter'). Here in John 14 and the subsequent chapters it is being used to talk of the ongoing work of the Holy Spirit in the lives of those who believe in Jesus to ensure that they are not abandoned in a world that is hostile to their faith. It is translated in a variety of ways, reflecting the depth of meaning to the word, but it could simply be rendered 'Helper' at this point. Jesus is promising that he will send them someone who will be to them just what he had been. He was the first 'Counsellor' or 'Helper' to his followers, but he cannot stay in the world any longer, so he will send a representative to take his place. But this replacement will not be some kind of second best who will leave us disappointed or let down. A friend of mine once described having to preach in the place of a well-known and popular speaker who had been taken ill only a couple of hours before a meeting. He said that there was an audible sigh of disappointment that rippled like a Mexican wave across the congregation as the announcement was made and people realized they were not going to get the preacher they had travelled to hear. There is no such disappointment, however, for us who receive the Holy Spirit. He is to us what Jesus would be because he is 'another Counsellor'—that is, another of the same kind, rather than another variety that might not be as good as the original.[2] If anything, we are better off.

Consider these advantages that Jesus mentions. The Spirit is always with us (John 14:17), so that we are not left like orphans by the absence of Jesus (that is, his physical absence that the disciples were evidently dreading). And while Jesus was limited to being with his disciples in one place, the presence of the Spirit means that he is with all of his followers all of the time. Moreover, he is closer to us now because he not only stands with us (as the meaning of the word 'Counsellor' indicates), but also lives in us (14:17). Not only alongside, but inside, too! This then makes it possible for Jesus to say that both he and his Father will make their home with those who obey his teaching (14:23; compare with 14:20). More than this, the Holy Spirit then acts as our teacher—a personal instructor for every believer—to guide us into an understanding of the truth and bring us to know Jesus more deeply (14:26; 16:13–14). We may not have Jesus physically with us, but the representative he has sent is, in essence, Jesus in another form.

The help the Spirit gives comes to us not only in these terms, but also produces a commodity much needed in times of stress—peace. Immediately after telling his disciples that he would send his Holy Spirit, Jesus says he will give them peace that nothing and no one else can provide (14:27). It is his parting gift to us and is one of the blessings we may expect to be given. If you think about it, peace can be taken away by other people or circumstances, but is not normally something which can be given. For instance, I may find peace under great difficulty and inspire others to believe it is possible to persevere under trial, but I cannot actually give that peace to anyone else. Great preachers may teach about the peace that comes through knowing Jesus and provide a huge boost to faith, but they cannot impart that peace. All they can do is point to the source and urge their hearers to search for it. But Jesus gives his peace— 'my peace'—to those who have the Holy Spirit. It is the peace that he experienced in a life of trust in God and willing obedience to his commands, even though that obedience cost him dearly. This he bestows freely on those who follow him in his path of obedience and trust and is further evidence that Jesus is not merely standing at a distance, hoping that we will come through in one piece. He is not just standing on the touchlines, shouting encouragement and advice. He lives within us by his Holy Spirit, so that his peace becomes ours.

> We may not have Jesus physically with us, but the representative he has sent is, in essence, Jesus in another form.

The God who is near

Moses asked a question that is relevant to us more than 3000 years later. 'What other nation is so great as to have their gods near them the way the LORD our God is near us whenever we pray to him?' (Deuteronomy 4:7). He will have had the immediate presence of God in mind, the fact that the Tent of Meeting stood in the centre of the Israelite camp, with pillar of cloud and fire towering over it, showing that God was with them at the same time as presenting the possibility of limited access to God every day. Impressive as that was, we have so much more.

Using Old Testament imagery, New Testament writers tell us that we may enter the most holy place, God's presence itself, that was off limits to all but the high priest, and even he could only go in once a year. As followers of Jesus Christ we have the right to approach God at any time. We do not need any mediator other than Jesus Christ himself, because he is both the high priest through whom we come to God, permanently residing in God's presence as our representative, and the sacrifice to remove sin that makes such an approach possible in the first place. In him we may approach God freely and with confidence that he will hear us and help us.

He lives within us by his Holy Spirit, so that his peace becomes ours.

God is not distant. He stands near to you as you trust him. Father, Son and Holy Spirit draw alongside you to comfort, encourage, strengthen, counsel and help you in the struggles you face. He has not left you to your own devices or turned away from you, but stands with you. His help is real, powerful and effective, so don't hesitate to ask him. To use an English idiom: Tea and cucumber sandwiches will not be served.

Summary: You have God both alongside and inside you.

Key verse: Hebrews 4:16: 'Let us then approach the throne of grace with confidence, so that we may receive mercy and find grace to help us in our time of need.'

To think about: In what way can you help others to know that God stands alongside them when life is tough?

'The LORD is good, a refuge in times of trouble', Nahum 1:7.

'The angel of the LORD encamps around those who fear him, and he delivers them', Psalm 34:7.

'At my first defence, no one came to my support, but everyone deserted me … But the Lord stood at my side and gave me strength … And I was delivered from the lion's mouth', 2 Timothy 4:16–17.

Thinking more deeply

Perhaps one of the most wonderful aspects of Jesus' promise to ask the Father to send another Counsellor (Paraclete) is that Jesus should bother to make the promise at all. He could have simply sent the Hoy Spirit without first being so solicitous of his disciples' confusion and grief. After all, it is Jesus who faces Gethsemane and the cross, not they. Yet here he consoles them: 'I will not leave you as orphans' (John 14:18)—without provision, without love, without a guardian and helper, without a protector and counsellor, without an explanation of these momentous events unfolding before their eyes. He promises 'I will come to you' (14:18)—not only at the end of the age, but in the Person of the Paraclete, the Holy Spirit sent as the successor of Jesus, and in many respects substitute for Jesus.

We cannot help but ask ourselves at this point if we worship God the Holy Spirit and accord him the reverence and love we owe and offer the Father and the Son. The successor Jesus has appointed is not ill-suited to his task. Far from it: he is to be to us what Jesus was to his own disciples during the days of his flesh. Let us worship and be thankful.

Don Carson, *Jesus and his Friends—His farewell message and prayer in John 14 to 17.*

Jesus joined the human race for a time so that he can now serve as our sympathetic advocate.

Philip Yancey, *Reaching for the Invisible God.*

Notes

1 Quoted in **John Stott,** *The message of Acts: to the ends of the earth* (The Bible Speaks Today series; Leicester: IVP, 1990), p. 42.

2 Those wishing to chase up the difference in the Greek between the two words for 'another' will find information in *Vine's Expository Dictionary of New Testament Words* (1989), p. 62.

11 Equipping:
All that you need

A complete resource for testing times

The Bible is no mere history book; it does things to people today (Jay Adams, How to help people change).

Please read 2 Timothy 3.

In some circles within the Christian community the impression is given that the Bible is nothing more than a great piece of ancient literature, an inspired book in which God spoke to his people in the past, but not one in which he speaks today. When troubles arise, then, such a book may provide examples of the strength believers have gained from knowing God, but it will not actually bring them face to face with this God so that they hear him addressing them about their own situation. For that something fresh is required, a high-octane spiritual experience which will connect the troubled believer directly to God, give a hotline to a divine answer and provide God's word now. But if this were the case, you would expect Paul to have something to say along these lines in this chapter, since he goes into some detail about life in a godless society and the persecution believers will experience as a result of wanting to follow Jesus, yet he doesn't. Instead he directs Timothy back to the Scriptures he was raised on.

Travelling through the storm

It is easy to see why advocates of the need for a supercharged encounter with God put their case as they do: 'There will be terrible times in the last days' (3:1). That phrase 'the last days' is not referring to an undetermined period of spiritual decline immediately prior to the return of the Lord Jesus, as if Paul is only describing what is going to happen at the end of time. If he were doing this we might think his words had little relevance to us. Rather, he is referring to the whole period between the ascension of the Lord and his return in glory, and is therefore describing life today and what society will, by and large, be like. His description, although put together nearly 2000 years ago, fits our society uncomfortably well, telling us (if we didn't know it already) that the world we live in can be a pretty dreadful place and will thus exert enormous pressure on any Christian who wants to remain faithful to the Lord. How can anyone withstand such a weight without fresh input straight from heaven?

Take the references in the list that have love as their focus: 'People will be lovers of themselves, lovers of money … without love … not lovers of the good … lovers of pleasure rather than lovers of God' (vv. 2–4). We like to think that we are more civilized than the Romans among whom Paul lived. After all we don't crucify criminals any more, or feed prisoners to the lions, but this list proves we are no further advanced in many other ways. People love all the wrong things (themselves, money, pleasure) and fail to love God or what is good, and the resultant behaviour fills out the rest of the list (boasting, pride, brutality, a lack of self-control and so on). It is inevitable that the Christian will, sooner or later, run into these features head on. If you are working for companies whose priority is profit (v. 2), then you are bound to clash with the money-grabbing your employers go in for, since they will be prepared to cut corners, diddle customers, make dishonest declarations about VAT—and you will not. I was once told in an interview, for a job I didn't get, that Christianity was an unrealistic philosophy for the business world where (and I paraphrase the colourful language of my interviewer) 'everybody is out to cheat everybody else'. Elsewhere a man told me in all seriousness that he could never become a Christian because he was a scrap metal dealer and all sorts of dubious stuff allegedly flies around in that line of work. I am not really in a position to comment about the scrap metal market, nor say whether all its dealers are dishonest, but it has always struck me that the man's comments are a perfect example of the problem facing the Christian. He recognized that his business was dodgy, but went along with it, accepting it as normal; the Christian, however, sees the dishonesty as evidence of a society ignoring what God wants and refuses to accept it as right. That can only cause problems for Christian employees, whose trust in God will be tested to the limit when confronted by competitors who use every trick in the book, accountants who sail close to the wind, colleagues and partners who swindle the company and customers who pay late.

If it wasn't enough for there to be terrible times in the world around us, life in the last days also affects the church and thus puts the squeeze on the followers of Christ in the very place they might think they are safe. Paul identifies some who have 'a form of godliness but denying its power' (3:5) and people like this have appeared down the ages in many guises. An old friend provided a perfect example when he described to me his upbringing in a Nonconformist church just after the First World War where the minister—a learned man—spent his Sunday sermons telling his very large congregation which parts of the Bible not to believe. Whether he realized it or not, the man was effectively disembowelling the faith of its vitals and leaving his congregation no possibility of growing a living trust in Christ. People still went to church (for a while, at least—the building is now closed), but there was no reality or power left. My friend said that, when he felt a call to go to the mission field, he knew he could not attend that denomination's training college as it would suck him dry. And this was by no means exceptional: nearly a whole denomination lost contact with the roots of the faith and withered. How can the faithful remain faithful under such pressure?

Today, evangelicals are not so much at risk from the liberalism that tore the heart out of the faith, as they are in danger from simply letting the heart die. With our culture's obsession with image, the temptation is to give more thought to the way the message is presented than to its content.

The 1960 American presidential campaign between John F. Kennedy and Richard Nixon was a defining moment in television history in this regard. For the first of their televised evening debates Kennedy shaved again and changed into clean clothes, while Nixon did neither of these, even refusing standard television make-up. The effect was dramatic. While political analysts said that they emerged pretty evenly on the content of the debate, image was the deciding factor. Kennedy appeared fresh and vital. Alongside him, Nixon looked haggard and weary. Telephone polls conducted after the debate confirmed that the majority of those who watched it would vote in favour of Kennedy. What is not usually known, according to the late journalist Alistair Cooke in one of his BBC radio broadcasts *Letter from America*, is that the same poll discovered that those who did not see the debate but listened to it on radio said they would vote by a similar margin in favour of Nixon.

This well-documented example of the triumph of presentation over content and style over substance now means that politicians have to polish their television image until it glows, since that is the place they will be seen most and judged by the population, and spin-doctors have to work overtime on putting the government's message across in a more palatable way. But will future generations look at evangelicals today and say they are guilty of the same? Will they see behind slick presentations a lack of trust in the Spirit of God? Will they conclude that we surrendered to the spirit of the age and were more preoccupied with the way we presented ourselves than with what we were actually saying? And will they say that we have prioritized image over content to the extent that content is not just sidelined, but lost altogether?

Whatever form it takes, a 'form of godliness' puts a throttling grip on true faith. It encourages people to think that external appearance is what really counts and so creates people whose desire for God is only superficial, something to make them look better. They do not want the real thing, they just wish to look as if they have it, because it is so much easier to dress up your religion with a facade of spirituality than actually struggle to grow and change on the inside. After all, cosmetic touch-ups are far less painful than heart surgery. But in any other circumstance, that is not called spin, it is called hypocrisy.

I don't know how many people I have met who have told me that they don't come to church because they think the place is full of hypocrites. My first flippant thought is that I should encourage them to come anyway, since one more won't make all that much difference, but I do realize there is a serious point behind their objection. In ancient Greek plays a 'hypocrite' was an actor who wore a mask, and mask-wearing can find its way into church behaviour, with people claiming to worship an all-seeing God using methods that are designed to conceal true motives from fellow worshippers (and perhaps even from God himself). But religious hypocrisy does not end with people showing off in church or emptying the faith of any serious content, and this is why it is so damaging. It will lead to a wholesale rejection of the truth. People who are godly only on the surface are not godly at all. Underneath they will be like the Pharisees, as Jesus described them: 'You clean the outside of the cup and dish, but inside they are full of greed and self-indulgence ... You are whitewashed tombs ... beautiful on the outside but on the inside ... full of dead men's bones and everything unclean ... On the outside you appear to people as righteous but on the inside you are full of hypocrisy and wickedness' (Matthew 23:25–28). So Paul shifts quite easily into describing the activities of those who use their empty religion to fill their pockets (3:6–9) and to persecute those who remain faithful to the Lord (3:10–12), and he ends with the sobering thought that because of people like this 'everyone who wants to live a godly life in Christ Jesus will be persecuted' (3:12).

Welcome to life in the last days! These 'terrible times' are perfectly usual features (normal, even) and should not take us by surprise, but they do place immense pressure on us as Christians because we are caught in the middle. If you are determined to stand firm for your faith you will run up against these obstacles. The big question then is: How are you going to cope? How will your faith withstand the test of living in this kind of world?

God's book meeting every eventuality

It is at this point that devotees of the need for a baptism of power (it goes under various names, depending on who you are talking to) come in with the answer you might have expected Paul to arrive at. Since life in the world is so tough and the church is not always what it should be, and taking into account all that we have been saying about the sometimes severe testing of faith that comes our way, the obvious need is for power from heaven in extra measure. Well, yes, and no.

It is always true to say that we need greater power from God to serve him adequately. No one who has the slightest awareness of the magnitude of the task facing them as a Christian in a hostile world or of his or her own weakness in the face of such hostility will disagree with that statement. Nor will I deny that it is possible for God to meet with his people in their extreme need, give wisdom, clear answers, deepened understanding and insight in a blinding flash. Of course that can happen—we know that it sometimes does—but there is no predefined pattern for such encounters. The most important question to ask is how God supplies these resources normally; and the bolt from the blue is not the usual way that we draw strength and wisdom from God. Which is why Paul directs Timothy in the crisis back to the Scriptures that will meet his every need: 'From infancy you have known the holy Scriptures, which are able to make you wise for salvation through faith in Christ Jesus. All Scripture is God-breathed and useful for teaching, rebuking, correcting and training in righteousness, so that the man of God may be thoroughly equipped for every good work' (2 Timothy 3:15–17).

The first feature of the Bible is that it is 'holy' (v. 15). Jay Adams says that there is a special significance in the word that is used. Instead of the more usual word *hagios* it is the word *hieros* that is employed. He writes,

The two terms ought probably to be distinguished in English by translating the first 'holy' and the second 'sacred'. Admittedly, the ideas are close, and the difference is subtle. *Hieros* is used to speak of the temple (the *hieron*) as the 'sacred place'. It means, essentially, that which is consecrated to God, that which is peculiarly associated with him. It speaks not of the character of the thing itself, but of its formal, external standing and relationship. That which is sacred is so because of its special, close attachment to God. As paper and ink, the Bible has no inherent dignity. But because of its association with the message it contains and the One whose Book it is, it is sacred. Like no other book, it is closely associated with God himself.[1]

> Like no other book, it is closely associated with God himself.

Since it is God's book and is so closely linked to him, it follows that it is going to be the place where we are most likely to find the help we need. The NIV translates Paul's words in verse 15 as 'which are able to make you wise …' but a more vivid translation (we even get our word 'dynamite' from the word used here) would be to say that the Scriptures 'have power' to do this. It was Charles Spurgeon who said that he would sooner defend a lion than the Bible, because he was convinced that it had a power all of its own to arrest people, bring them up short and transform them. That is why some of the most effective evangelistic methods revolve around getting people face-to-face with what the Scriptures say, since it puts them within reach of what God has to say to them. For the same reason, when you are under pressure or unable to understand what God is doing in your life, the biggest mistake you could make would be to cut yourself off from such a powerful resource. Don't keep the lion caged up!

This close association with God is further amplified when Paul describes Scripture as 'God-breathed.' That translation is a very helpful rendering of a compound word in the Greek used to describe the process by which the Scriptures came to us. We sometimes speak of writers pouring their heart and soul into what they write, so that the finished work is not only a piece of them, but also speaks for them. When you read their work, you hear their voices, you feel their passion as if they were addressing you personally. Here Paul describes the Scriptures coming as a result of God speaking out and breathing over the writers, so that the resultant work carries his presence and voice with it. While it was written by human authors, it is *his* word because he has poured himself into its pages. He speaks in it, not just to previous generations, but also addressing you and me personally today through it (look for instance at the use of the present tense in Hebrews 3:7—quoting an Old Testament psalm, the writer prefaces the quote with 'As the Holy Spirit says …', not just 'said'). It is 'the living and enduring word of God' (1 Peter 1:23) that will always be relevant for each generation in every part of the world, whatever is happening to them. God is speaking today!

> The biggest mistake you could make would be to cut yourself off from such a powerful resource. Don't keep the lion caged up!

Since it is God who is speaking to us in the Scriptures Paul says that the Bible is 'useful', a rare piece of apostolic understatement if there ever was one. It basically helps in every area of life that we could ever think of: 'teaching' us what God's will is; 'rebuking' when we stray; 'correcting' the wrong behaviour, which includes showing how to get back on the right track; and 'training in righteousness', giving a framework for life so that we please God. The NIV rather weakens the impact of the concluding part of the sentence—'so that the man of God may be thoroughly equipped for every good work'—by compressing two of Paul's words into one phrase. 'Thoroughly equipped' comes firstly from a word meaning 'able to meet all demands', which is combined with another word referring to the fitting out of a ship so that it has everything required for the voyage. You have everything you need!

Fitted out for the voyage

If you are a worrier you will know that sense of unexplained dread there can be about going on a journey. Have you remembered to pack everything? Is there anything you have forgotten? Are you likely to encounter unforeseen circumstances that will expose your preparation as inadequate? And the anxiety is not lessened even when you know that you can probably buy what you have left behind when you arrive, because there is always the possibility that you might not be able to. There is little anyone else can do to reassure you in such circumstances.

While it was written by human authors, it is his word because he has poured himself into its pages.

But you can do something about that unnamed dread that you might not be equipped for the tests of faith or the storms of life. These storms are rather like parenthood: nothing you do will completely prepare you for the events that burst in on you, but you are not utterly helpless. A life that is lived in close harmony with God and his Word will be a life that is fitted out for the journey, whatever that journey holds. The ship may ride some enormous waves and even look as if it is in danger of capsizing and sinking, but it will ride out the storm because it has been prepared properly.

It is ironic then, tragic even, that with such a resource to hand, Christians still hanker for something else—something more immediate, perhaps, or maybe more relevant, or possibly just something more exciting than the plain old Bible? But in doing so they fail to realize the awesome extent of the resource they have already been provided with. Indeed, a preoccupation with the spectacular and exciting works against them appreciating what they already have. But perhaps it is already too late to sound this warning.

The Bible Society has been saying for a number of years that the majority of Christians do not look at their Bibles from one week to the next. Even in evangelical meetings it is not always obvious that we are Bible believers. I once attended a missionary meeting which was attended by several hundred young people. The meeting was lively and stimulating, but reference was made more frequently to the original founder's sayings than to the Bible. In fact, the Bible was mentioned in passing only once and the talk was nothing more than a pre-packed evangelistic summary that appears in many tracts. It was neither excitingly presented nor even relevant to the theme of the evening. The speaker himself admitted that he did not feel especially qualified to address the meeting since he only ran the bookstall, but no effort had been made to obtain a good speaker from one of the many evangelical churches in the city—and yet we were told that the music group who led the worship (and played well) had been fetched from over seventy miles away. The overall impression of the evening was that world mission was a good thing (and it is), but the absence of the Bible meant that it came over as one of our better ideas, rather than God's. Moreover, the opportunity was lost to let the Word of God speak about it, direct the excitement these young people felt and equip them for the task they had been hearing about.

Will the Bible be read … or will it just sit in the background?

I wonder how exceptional this meeting was; I suspect it reflects the way many churches (and believers) treat the Bible. What sort of sermon will you hear if you go to an evangelical church this weekend? A message where the Bible is allowed to speak, or a three point sermon in which the preacher has decided what to say before looking for a text to hang it on? Will the Bible be read (remember that, in addition to commanding the teaching of Scripture, Paul told Timothy to devote himself to the public reading of Scripture—virtually everything else we crowd into our services is optional), or will it just sit in the background?

It is no good in the background. Household items that are not used tend to sit on the shelf for years before they are moved. Everyone knows they are there, and feels slightly guilty about not using them, but they remain undisturbed until they are eventually put in the back of a cupboard. Years later they are found again and moved to a box in the loft, before finally going out to a jumble sale. A Bible in the background will suffer the same fate: we know it's there, but it's doing nothing useful and, even though we know we ought to do something more with it, sooner or later it will be discarded altogether.

But if the Bible is the only place we are guaranteed to hear God's voice and is the only source that will give us everything we need for faith in today's world, it must instead be at the heart of everything we do. To paraphrase something I said earlier: Since life in the world is so tough and the church is not always what it should be, and taking into account all that we have been saying about the sometimes severe testing of faith that comes our way, how can we go anywhere else?

Summary: In the Scriptures you come face-to-face with God and hear him speak.

Key verses: 2 Timothy 3:15–17: 'From infancy you have known the holy Scriptures, which are able to make you wise for salvation through faith in Christ Jesus. All Scripture is God-breathed and is useful for teaching, rebuking, correcting and training in righteousness, so that the man of God may be thoroughly equipped for every good work.'

To think about: Why do we find it so difficult to read the Bible consistently and regularly? What can we do to help one another with this problem?

'No prophecy of Scripture came about by the prophet's own interpretation. For prophecy never had its origin in the will of man, but men spoke from God as they were carried along by the Holy Spirit', 2 Peter 1:20–21.

'You have been born again, not of perishable seed, but of imperishable, through the living and enduring word of God', 1 Peter 1:23.

Thinking more deeply

The Bible was written in tears and to tears it will yield its treasures. God has nothing to say to the frivolous man.

A.W. Tozer, *God tells the man who cares.*

Looking back over this chapter as a whole, we can appreciate the relevance of its message to our pluralist and permissive society. The 'times of stress' in which we seem to be living are very distressing. Sometimes one wonders if the world and the church have gone mad, so strange are their views, and so lax their standards. Some Christians are swept from their moorings by the floodtide of sin and error. Others go into hiding, as offering the best hope of survival, the only alternative to surrender. But neither of these is the Christian way. 'But as for you,' Paul says to us as he did to Timothy, 'stand firm. Never mind if you are young, inexperienced, timid and weak. Never mind if you find yourself alone in your witness. You have followed my teaching so far. Now continue in what you have come to believe. You know the biblical credentials of your faith. Scripture is God-breathed and profitable. Even in the midst of these grievous times in which evil men and impostors go from bad to worse, it can make you complete and it can equip you for your work. Let the word of God make you a man of God! Remain loyal and it will lead you on into Christian maturity.'

John Stott, *Guard the Gospel: The message of 2 Timothy.*

Notes

1 **Jay Adams,** *How to help people change* (Grand Rapids: Zondervan, 1986), p. 22.

12 Transformation:
Grand designs

God's ultimate aim

It is God's plan that his people should become like his Son, not that they should muddle along in a modest respectability (Leon Morris, Commentary on Romans).

Please read Romans 8:28–39.

Where would the Christian calendar market be without breathtaking pieces like Romans 8? Purple passages like this one are a fertile soil for texts for posters and calendars, and it is not hard to see why, when there is so much that is positive and uplifting. Take one of these verses and add it to a picture of a mellow autumn scene in New England, or fishing boats in a Scottish harbour bathed in warm sunshine, and you have a heavenly combination to hang on the kitchen wall that will soothe the troubled spirit.

But we ought to have a different sort of picture. Suppose you used one of the same Scottish harbour at the height of a January gale, with a lowering sky and the fishing fleet tossed by a mountainous sea? Perhaps that would not convey much in the way of the unruffled calm the calendars normally aim to portray, but it would more accurately reflect the circumstances under which these lines were penned and under which they had to be believed by those to whom they were addressed. It is possible to gain the impression that, metaphorically speaking, Paul was in the June sunshine as he wrote, seated on the harbour wall with his watercolours, writing and

They are bright promises to shine in dark skies, a source of strength for times of testing.

illustrating his latest devotional anthology. In reality he was in a stricken boat in the middle of a tempest.

Why, for instance, does Paul make the point that God is working in all things for the good of those who love him? Precisely because all the things they were facing were so terrible that it looked as if he wasn't. Why are there all those 'Who can be against us?' questions and answers? Because everybody was against them! Why are those two frightful lists recorded at the end of the section? Because that is just what was happening to them. These verses were written in anything but tranquil surroundings and are therefore ideally suited to build assurance of God's love in the storm. They are bright promises to shine in dark skies, a source of strength for times of testing.

Just three verses are of interest to us here, verses 28–30, since they provide both comfort and challenge. Within these lines there are clear indications of what God is doing in our lives at those times we feel most abandoned and what his intentions are for us as he leads us through such testing circumstances.

In all things

The conviction of Romans 8:28 is that God works in and through all circumstances you and I face. This is something we must never forget, because there will be many times when it looks as if God is completely absent. This verse is a promise of God's special assistance for those who belong to him, addressing believers with the assurance of his particular grace towards them because they love him and have been called by him. God is working in your life for good, so that you are not at the mercy of fate or chance, which in common parlance is often expressed by people saying something like 'It will work out for the best.' Events do not just work out all by themselves. God takes them and uses them for the good. It is his guiding hand, and not some impersonal fate, that moulds and shapes the seemingly disastrous into the beneficial. Paul indicates that God is directing events at every point and urges you to place wholehearted trust in him.

> Events do not just work out all by themselves. God takes them and uses them for the good.

In all things God works for your good; that is, however, not the same as saying that all things will be good. Perhaps the greatest misunderstanding lies here. Christians can take this to mean that God will not allow anything bad to happen to them and thus they come unstuck when something terrible does happen. But nowhere has God given his people promises of immunity from suffering and he does not do so here, either. Christian suffering is a reality. What he does guarantee is that he will work in and through all events to *bring* good. All that we regard as most catastrophic, hopeless, unredeemable—and we have seen plenty of examples in previous chapters that fit that description—he will take and use for the good. He will work in and through the evil that is inflicted on us by others; he will work likewise in the evil we may do to others, bringing good even from our sins; and when we are struck down without warning, he will be there to repair the damage. Not that you will necessarily be able to see that at the time; you will probably have to take it on trust that, in the building work which God is doing in your life, no material is unusable.

Where is it all heading?

At this point the observant will come in with an awkward question: just what does Paul mean by 'good'? Awkward, perhaps, but a valid question nonetheless. When the *Herald of Free Enterprise* capsized in Zeebrugge harbour in March 1987 with the loss of nearly 200 lives one of the questions that was debated on a radio broadcast was where the good lay in such terrible events. The question was, however, not answered satisfactorily because those involved in the discussion were ill-informed about just what was meant by 'good'. Popular interpretation of this concept is probably led by tabloid understanding: it can only be good if it ends with the guy getting the girl (and a pretty one at that), winning untold riches and being able to afford to buy a mansion with twenty-four bedrooms and 300 acres of parkland—and there wasn't anything of that when the ship sank. You don't need me to tell you that this is not what God has in mind as good.

Or perhaps you do. The good that God desires for us is so radically different from the good that most of our world aspires to, that it may come as a huge surprise to discover exactly what Paul means by 'good'. The next verse supplies the answer: 'to be conformed[1] to the likeness of his Son' (8:29). To use an English word that is related to the Greek, metamorphosis is what God is looking for, so that we change to be more like Christ.

God's aim is to make you and me like his Son, Jesus Christ, and all his work in our lives has that goal in mind. We blandly imagine that God's only interest is in bailing us out of the mess we are in and taking us to heaven, but he has much higher (and harder) things in mind. He could remain content with merely completing the transformation at the end of our lives. Indeed, we know that he is going to do that—for instance, John tells us in 1 John 3:2 that 'when he appears, we shall be like him' and Paul in Philippians 3:21 says that he will 'transform our lowly bodies so that they will be like his glorious body'; both these are only talking about the very end. But what Paul in Romans seems to be describing is a process that carries on throughout our lives: God works in all things with the ultimate end in view, which he has planned for us from eternity, that we should be conformed to the likeness of his Son, Jesus Christ. God has brought us into his family, so he insists that we bear a family likeness. In the difficulties we encounter, therefore, the 'good' is not necessarily that the troubles should cease, but that we should grow in them so that we are forged in the same mould as Christ, the elder Brother of the family, becoming like him as much as we can.

> God's aim is to make you and me like his Son, Jesus Christ, and all his work in our lives has that goal in mind.

This is an altogether different proposition. It would be a comparatively easy prospect just to wait for death to effect the great change. We could then shamble through life just as we pleased, not worrying about growth, content to wait for death to make us what God wanted all at once. Rather like facing surgery, the painful stuff would be done while we slept and we would wake up transformed. But if the transformation process begins here, then we are facing something far more protracted and difficult.

Paul has some revealing words in Galatians 4:19 about this process: 'My dear children, for whom I am in the pains of childbirth until Christ is formed in you ...' Using a word that is related to the term in Romans, Paul has this Christian metamorphosis in view, and his problem as he writes to the Galatian church is that he doesn't see it taking place the way it should, so he has some strong things to say to his readers. What is so startling about his comment here is the metaphor he uses: the process of growing people in Christ is something akin to giving birth. I mentioned earlier that I was present at the birth of all three of our children—I discovered that it is not called labour for nothing! If that is the picture Paul uses for pastoral work, is there any wonder it can be so agonizingly painful at times? But the metaphor also sheds light on the process itself and demonstrates that growing in Christ is far from straightforward. It is a long, hard struggle.

There is sometimes a naivety about the way some preachers think that all they have to do is declare the word of God, tell it like it is and people will joyfully embrace it and allow it to mould their lives. But it comes as a rather rude shock to preachers that Christians can be so resistant to what God has to say, all of which demonstrates that bringing human nature— even redeemed human nature—into line with Christ is no mean task. To say that there is a rebellious streak within all of us is hardly adequate. Every aspect of human nature is tainted and twisted by sin, so that all our actions have an anti-God bias that both tries to shut him out and damages our relationships with fellow human beings. Becoming a Christian does not magically straighten everything out. The straightening-out process we call sanctification, and it takes a lifetime. If you have been a Christian for more than a couple of years you will be able to think of incidents which uncovered ingrained sin that you would never have guessed was present beforehand. Somebody's actions towards you bring to the surface bitterness you had forgotten about; or when under pressure you fly into a rage. The essence of humbling discoveries such as these is the realization that you are not as Christlike as you had previously assumed and that there is still a lot that needs changing. But such discoveries do not cease after five, ten or even twenty years, they go on right to the end. The struggle is not finished until we step into eternity.

> Bringing human nature—even redeemed human nature—into line with Christ is no mean task.

Our greatest good?

Of course, you need to be convinced that being conformed to the likeness of Jesus Christ is something that actually is good, that the highest and best aim God can have for us is that we should be like his Son and that this war of attrition on sinful human nature to bring it about is worthwhile. If you have accepted the tabloid definition of 'good' (getting the girl, etc.) then this will seem like a joke, and a rather bad one at that. We go through fire and water for this? And how can you measure growth in Christian character, anyway? But looking at it from God's point of view, there can be nothing higher for him to bestow upon us.

Our sin separates us from God, so the best that God can do will reconcile us to him, because if we remain separated from him we will be eternally unhappy. In salvation we are brought into Christ and clothed with his perfection, so that we are accepted in Christ and when God looks at us he sees Christ. The highest good to which we can therefore attain is to grow to be more like Christ, since that will bring us closer to God and his love.

> The highest and best aim God can have for us is that we should be like his Son.

There is nothing greater than this, so all of God's involvement in our lives will direct us towards this goal. Material prosperity is not his central concern, nor even our health and happiness, although he may give us those things. Difficulties and trials that come our way have as their focus the driving out of natural and sinful tendencies and the growth of character that is as much like Jesus as it is possible to be this side of eternity.

It is easy to say this, but how do we know that all this will actually achieve the desired metamorphosis? Or that God will not lose patience with the stragglers and simply leave them behind? We know it because God has guaranteed it himself.

Complete security

Romans 8:29–30 is made up of a list of five significant words. Grasp these and you will understand God's determination both to save and transform you. Each word centres on what God has done (there is no room in them for any human activity which would make the final outcome uncertain) and together they form an unbreakable chain, anchored at each end in eternity, that holds the Christian in complete security. They open up the secret world of the counsels of God in eternity to state what went on to bring you to faith, and guarantee that God will then bring you—transformed—to heaven. All five words are written in the past tense: they are so certain that, from God's perspective, they have already happened.

It begins with 'those God *foreknew*.' Foreknowledge is often thought of only as God knowing in advance what each person's response would be to him and who would believe in him. But the word is not saying God knew what people would do in advance; it says he knew certain people in advance. Leon Morris in his commentary on these verses in Romans thinks that the best way to understand the word is 'to choose[2] in advance.'[3] You will see the same idea in Jeremiah 1:5 where God says 'Before I formed you in the womb I knew you; before you were born I set you apart.' There, God's knowledge of Jeremiah is linked to his choosing the young man for the role of being a prophet to Israel, and the same meaning is in view in Romans. God knew you before you were born and loved you even then as one of his own.

> Rather he has determined in advance that his people will be moulded into the likeness of Christ, and will certainly bring it about.

'Those … he also *predestined* to be conformed to the likeness of his Son.' According to Leon Morris, the term 'predestined' means to 'set the boundary beforehand', indicating that there is nothing which will prevent God from completing the transformation we have been thinking about.[4] Businesses may establish production targets, railway companies tell you they hope to have 98% of their trains arrive on time, workers plan for retirement, but none can actually guarantee any of these things will happen. But what Paul has described is not merely a desire or aim, something that God would like to see happen, 'all things being equal', as we say. Rather he has determined in advance that his people will be moulded into the likeness of Christ, and will certainly bring it about.

'And those he predestined, he also *called*.' Having determined to see you transformed into the likeness of Christ, God called you to himself. It was probably through a friend's explanation of the gospel, or perhaps a church service, that you first heard the Christian message, but behind it and through it God was speaking. It was his Spirit that opened your heart to understand the good news and receive Christ to ensure that this great work in your life actually began.

'Those he called, he also *justified*.' It would be fair to say that many of our worries would be dispelled if we could gain a fuller understanding of the riches contained in this word. We can only approach God if we are righteous in his sight. Those who have been justified have God's official declaration that Jesus has paid the penalty for their sins by dying on the cross, so that their sins are removed altogether. They stand accepted in Christ, clothed with his perfection, declared by God to be not guilty. This heartening chapter in Romans begins with the statement that 'there is now no condemnation for those who are in Christ Jesus', and ends with the affirmation that there is nothing in all creation that 'will be able to separate us from the love of God that is in Christ Jesus our Lord' and justification is the key reason for this. No condemnation before God. No separation from God. The next word is inevitable.

'Those he justified, he also *glorified*.' This final word anchors the chain back in eternity, since it speaks of God taking his people to be with him, but is rather surprisingly put. We would naturally expect Paul, when talking about what is a future event for us, to say 'and he *will* also glorify them.' But he has put it in the past tense. For God it is not a future event, but one that has already happened in his sight. It is as certain for God as those things that have already taken place. Difficult though the process may be, you need have no doubt about God's intention of bringing the work to completion. You and I are as good as there!

Final assurance in trials

In previous chapters we have seen the many ways in which testing circumstances come upon those who are looking to follow Jesus Christ. Some of these have been scary, to say the least, since they involve events that may threaten faith itself. These five words offer, therefore, the much-needed assurance that those trials will not destroy faith. Behind them lies the will and purpose of a God who has saved us for himself and will not let us be separated from him. His aim through all of life, and therefore also in these trials, is to refine character and create people who bear the image and likeness of his Son Jesus Christ. That is a staggeringly high aim and would be too much to ask of any one of us if God had not already determined to accomplish it himself. Happily for us, he declares his intention here of finishing what he has started and that nothing will put him off.

Summary: God's aim for my life is nothing less than to transform me so that I become like his Son.

Key verse: Romans 8:29: 'For those God foreknew he also predestined to be conformed to the likeness of his Son.'

To think about: What assurance do you gain from Romans 8:29–30 that the testing of your faith will not harm you, but actually help you grow in Christ?

'Those … in Christ Jesus and called to be holy …', 1 Corinthians 1:2.

'He chose us in him before the creation of the world to be holy and blameless in his sight. In love he predestined us to be adopted as his sons through Jesus Christ …' Ephesians 1:4–5.

Thinking more deeply

In extending encouragement and support to the people of God in their sufferings and adversities, groanings and infirmities, the apostle has reached this triumphant conclusion. He has shown how the present pilgrimage of the people of God falls into its place in that determinate and undefeatable plan of God that is bounded by two foci, the sovereign love of God in his eternal counsel and glorification with Christ in the age to come. It is when they apprehend by faith this panorama that stretches from the love of God before times eternal to the grand finale of the redemptive process, that the sufferings of this present time are viewed in their true perspective and are seen [from the perspective of eternity] to be but

the circumstances of pilgrimage to, and preconditions of, a glory to be revealed so great in its weight that the tribulations are not worthy of comparison.
John Murray, *Commentary on Romans* (8:30).

The first thirty verses [of Romans 8] set forth *the adequacy of the grace of God* to deal with a whole series of predicaments—the guilt and power of sin (verses 1–9); the fact of death (verses 6–13); the terror of confronting God's holiness (verse 15); weakness and despair in the face of suffering (verses 17–25); paralysis in prayer (verses 26f.); the feeling that life is meaningless and hopeless (verses 28–30). Paul also makes his point by dwelling on four gifts of God given to all who by faith are 'in Christ Jesus'. The first is *righteousness*—'no condemnation' (verse 1). The second is *the Holy Spirit* (verses 4–27). The third is *sonship*—adoption into the divine family in which the Lord Jesus is the firstborn (verses 14–17,29). The fourth is *security*, now and for ever (verses 28–30). This composite endowment—a status, plus a dynamic, plus an identity, plus a safe-conduct—is more than enough to support a Christian whatsoever his trouble.
J.I. Packer, *Knowing God*.

Notes

1 *Vine's Expository Dictionary of New Testament Words* says that the word *summorphos* (translated here as 'conformed') signifies having the same form as another.
2 The AV translates Amos 3:2 as 'You only have I *known* of all the families of the earth.' The NIV renders this word 'known' as 'chosen', demonstrating the close link between the concepts.
3 **Leon Morris,** *The Epistle to the Romans* (Leicester: IVP, 1988), p. 332.
4 **Morris,** *Romans*, p. 332 (footnote).

13 Hope:
A fourth man in the flames

Meeting God in the furnace

Suffering has a constructive purpose. 'They will call on my name.' As a result of all they have experienced they find their true identity in relationship with the Lord, for they call on him and he claims them as his own (Joyce Baldwin, Commentary on Zechariah).

Please read Zechariah 13:7–9.

When the prophet Daniel's three friends were thrown into the furnace for refusing to bow down to the Babylonian king Nebuchadnezzar's image, there were two surprises in store for everyone at court that day. The first was that the three were not consumed by the flames. Intense as the heat was, they were not even singed when they emerged. And the second was to see that God was closer to them in the fire than at any other time. Three men were cast into the inferno, but a fourth appeared alongside them, one who looked, in the king's words, 'like a son of the gods' (Daniel 3:25).

These men's experience in many ways mirrors what happens when believers go through great difficulty and trial. While it would not be right to conclude from this that Christians will always be preserved intact, they are nevertheless frequently enabled to bear up under great strain and demonstrate a peace that is so evidently not from themselves that it causes amazement and even disbelief in both onlookers and persecutors. That they are able to do this is because they have discovered the presence of God in the flames in a way that they did not know him previously—and perhaps could not. They have known him standing alongside them, heard his voice and felt his strengthening hand, so that they emerge stronger and more confident in God.

Zechariah 13:9 expresses this unexpected result in quite touching words as the prophet depicts God's people going through a series of devastating events. The shepherd is struck and the sheep are scattered. The nation is decimated and the remnant sent through the fire to be refined and tested, but something significant happens. They draw near to God and he draws near to them. In the midst of the flames 'they … call on my name and I … answer them.' Far from being abandoned in their extremity, they find him near and glad to own them as his: 'They are my people.' Hearing this draws out a response of love from his beleaguered disciples: 'The LORD is our God.' They discover that he is both everything they need and everything they want.

This verse seems to encapsulate the mystery of the testing of faith that this book has been attempting to outline. The sort of events we have been considering in previous chapters do not drive people away from God, but into his arms. The relationship is not weakened by what happens, but rather made stronger. Zechariah's words therefore bring us full circle. We began with James' instructions to count trials and testing as joy because there is great reward in standing firm. Here Zechariah puts that reward in beautifully simple terms that make joy an understandable outcome. In painful trials God draws near to bring comfort with the assurance, spoken deep into the soul, that they belong to him, that he stands with them, and that nothing which has happened in any way casts doubt upon their acceptance with him: 'They are my people.' It is the assurance the believer longs to hear at any time, but especially in troubles. Job did not know what God was doing, but refused to believe his friends' assertions that God must be punishing him. In his despair he argued passionately with them, while at the same time calling out to God to answer him. In the end he got his answer as God spoke out of the storm, and Job was satisfied. God confirmed that Job was right and stood with Job. Job had nothing to say, but bowed in worship: 'The Lord is [my] God.'

I do not mean to suggest that the trials suddenly become easier once we appreciate this. No. It is, as we have seen, in the very nature of trials to be hard and God's faithful followers will make mistakes as they face them. Remember that Hezekiah stood alone and succumbed to the temptation of joining the Babylonian revolt rather than trusting God to preserve his kingdom from the Assyrians, but we also saw that God did not abandon him. He still saw God's deliverance when the Assyrians laid siege to Jerusalem, a demonstration almost without equal of God owning the Israelite's as his people, that he was standing with them in the fire. And Hezekiah's response was one of exuberant and triumphant praise at having experienced the delivering power of God so close at hand: 'The Lord is our God!'

In each of the scenarios sketched out in previous chapters—whether Paul's setbacks, Joseph's meandering course, or Jeremiah's disappointments—believers faced circumstances that stretched faith to breaking point and we must expect it to be no different for us. That might sound like a good reason for a morbid and gloomy approach to life, but it is just the opposite. There is hope. Doubtless we will stumble as we struggle to deal with testing circumstances, but this will affect neither the help we receive while they last nor their long-term outcome. God will be present in the flames, whether we see him or not. His Word will speak to us and his Spirit will comfort and strengthen us. Standing with us he will own us as his children, speaking his peace into our lives in ways that will both humble and thrill us. And, even though we might not feel like it immediately, there will come a time when we will learn to view our trials from his perspective, see how they bring us closer to him and even accept them with—dare I say it—joy.

Summary: I may experience God more closely in severe trials than at any other time.

Key verse: Zechariah 13:9: 'This third I will bring into the fire; I will refine them like silver and test them like gold. They will call on my name and I will answer them; I will say, "They are my people," and they will say, "The LORD is our God".'

To think about: How have you experienced God's presence in difficulties in a way that strengthened your faith in him?